HOW TO CONSERVE
CONSERVATIONISTS

How to Conserve Conservationists

2nd Edition

JESSIE PANAZZOLO

Lonely Conservationists

CONTENTS

EDITOR

Edited by Renuka Kulkarni
A fellow lonely conservationist

This book is dedicated to both my community of lonely conservationists and all of the people who have ever genuinely supported me on my conservation journey. Your empowering words, listening ears and open hearts have carried me through the rollercoaster of experiences and emotions that I have faced over the past two decades. Without people like you in my life, who knows, I may not have made it this far to be able to tell my story.

| 1 |

Why do we need to conserve conservationists anyway?

Conservationists Anonymous

On the 29th of January 2019, I was lying on my couch and letting my mind wander to a fictional self-help meeting in my mind. In my vision, I sat among others in the imaginary circle of chairs with the faint aroma of *Arnott's* assorted biscuits and instant coffee wafting in the background. You must keep in mind that I have never actually been to a real community group help session of any kind, so I can only go off of what I have seen portrayed on TV and in movies. The group facilitator nods at me, and so I introduce myself.

"My name is Jessie and I am the loneliest conservationist in the world."

The group choruses back.

"HeLLo, JEssIE."

Before this session could continue, a buzz in my pocket snapped me out of it. It was a friend of mine from Spain who I had formally met in Malaysia. I was there learning all about elephants in preparation for my honours degree, which had a strong focus on elephant ecology. This friend of mine was phenomenal at what she did and I loved her enthusiasm when she talked about her work. Unfortunately, she often had undertones of self-doubt in her voice as everyone else working within in the project was doing a PhD, Master's degree, or was a local Malaysian research assistant.

This particular message from my friend wasn't about these feelings, but her message did express other notions of uncertainty. She told me that she was stuck in Spain while waiting for her visa to be approved so she could go back to Malaysia to continue her work. This perfectly timed message was enough to snap me out of the delusion that I was the loneliest conservationist in the world and in that moment, I wondered how many other lonely conservationists were out there.

A lifetime chasing dreams

To give some context as to why I felt like the loneliest conservationist in the world, I was experiencing burnout after an entire lifetime spent chasing my conservation-oriented dreams. When I was three years old, I was handed a stuffed toy gorilla by my mother who returned home from Canada, of all places, which set me on a life-long journey of discovery fuelled by a determination to protect the natural world. By the time I was five years old, I was asking my mum how I could save my gorilla's cousin, the orangutan, from habitat destruction. I couldn't understand why my life was governed by such strict rules when the adults who were chopping down rainforests weren't held to the same rigour. It was then that I realised that my parents didn't know all the answers and I set off on the rest of my life, trying to figure out where it all went wrong for great apes.

Blinkers on, school and university went by as I forged my way toward the answers. By the time I was 24, I was finally conducting research on orangutans and elephants in a newly restored North Sumatran forest that was formally oil palm plantations. I was finally living my dream, so why did it feel so wrong?

I looked around at the mothers growing saplings with their children in the nursery, and the fathers watering the freshly planted trees in the earth. There was a cultural and economic shift towards growing sustainable livelihoods which led to new knowledge and behaviours being passed on from generation to generation all around me. Suddenly I was hit with the truth: I didn't belong in the forest if I truly believed in sustainable or long-term change for this ecosystem. As soon as my research was over, I packed my bags and headed home to Australia.

Back in Australia, I felt lost. I had spent my entire life focused on one conservation dream, and I had to give it up so suddenly. With the dream, I gave up the foothold in the industry that I had spent all of my time building: contacts, a reputation and opportunities. I tried volunteering and working for various businesses around Australia, starting from the beginning and trying to apply my skills to energy saving, zoo education and koala conservation. A lack of funding, abusive bosses and isolation seemed to cycle through my life, and like waves lapping at a big strong cliff face, over time, my passion and drive wore away.

The straw that broke the camel's back

My last straw was an attempt at commonly distributed advice which was to volunteer for a large conservation NGO until I proved myself to them, leading them to add me to payroll. Six months of full-time office work, complex report writing and data analysis later, I found myself at a cafe with one of the staff members who was hiring for an upcoming position. I couldn't believe it when they told me that I didn't have enough experience to take the job, even as they continued to extend the applications for a length of time that they could have spent training me in my knowledge gaps. The following weekend I stared solemnly at my placemat after my friend Tim served me dinner. He explained his knowledge of the NGO and how they would never pay me as long as I continued to work for free. I felt like I had no hope of establishing myself in the conservation industry anymore, I had tried everything I could think of and more. I never returned to that office again.

So, there I was on the following Monday, lying on my

couch imagining that I was at a group therapy session and truly believing that I was the only person on Earth who had experienced the groundhog days of the conservation industry. Time and time again, giving my all, proving my value, and being left to the side feeling worthless, but having to muster the energy to start again. I was exhausted and I felt like there was nothing more I could offer to the industry that could change the way I was perceived. I had an honours degree, I had worked and volunteered for multiple organisations, I had presented at many conferences and had even won awards for my research. None of it seemed to be enough.

Speaking out

There is no doubt in my mind that I was done with the industry at that point, as no conservationist speaks her truth if she has something to lose. The stakes were too high in the industry and the cost was too great with so few jobs available and so many incredible candidates to choose from. When I got that message from my Spanish friend, I was inspired to find out the truth, or at least tell my truth. I got up, walked to my desk, and created a blog that I titled *Lonely Conservationists* and just started writing. Another friend suggested I make an Instagram page to promote the blog of the same name and so I did. I hit publish on both platforms and waited for either nothing to happen or for an onslaught of heckles about how I was so entitled or someone who just didn't try hard enough to make it in the industry.

What I never expected was the 50 blogs that I accumulated from other global conservationists over the rest of that year, and the weekly blogs that continued to flood into the proceeding years every Wednesday. I didn't anticipate the Instagram page to form a community of thousands of others who also dubbed themselves *Lonely Conservationists* and who formed their own localised communities over shared interests or location. The comradery and the *"Me too!"* that constantly echoed in our minds as we read each other's stories was a feeling I could never predict. The wonderful plot twist was that although I never got that job with the NGO, I still found my calling that year.

In starting this community, I made the transition from conservationist to a *'conservationist conservationist'* and I learnt so much about the way we feel, the way we are treated, and the way we share experiences, no matter where in the world we live, study and work. It is not just me or even just Australian conservationists that can relate to the struggle. It turns out that there are conservationists from hundreds of countries across the world who share my experiences and frustration in creating a career for themselves.

From seed to seedling

From its angsty but humble beginnings in 2019 to the time of writing in 2021, *Lonely Conservationists* has grown in leaps and bounds. *Lonely Conservationists* has become a pioneering platform in empowering conservationists and has produced a range of educational content about the lived experiences of conservationists from our blogs, to education programs, webinars, a podcast and books. I have been fortunate enough to be able to represent *Lonely Conservationists* in many international conferences, including speaking at the Earth Optimism Summit for the Smithsonian Institute in 2020 and being sponsored as a Women in STEM Changemaker at the Australian Academy of Science gender equity conference in 2019. I have worked and continue to work with international scientists to add to the data pool of research on the conservationist experience and have collaborated with businesses, NGOs and passionate individuals around the world. Well-known journals like Australian Geographic and Mongabay have written about the community and I have been given the opportunity to speak on national radio stations such as the ABC. In a twist of events that I could never predict, I made a career for myself out of admitting that I was struggling to find one.

After fostering the community, building relationships with other like-minded professionals, and providing a platform for unheard voices, it has become imperative that I pass on some of what I have learnt to others. I am positive that by doing so, some of this knowledge can help people like the Jessie of the past who felt very undervalued, burnt out, and frustrated with her time navigating the industry. It must be noted, however, that this book is not just for struggling conservationists, but it is probably more useful for everyone else to read. The people who are outside of the industry, but may have conservationists in their lives, or people who have established themselves in the industry and have forgotten what it's like to be early on in their career. I think this book would be useful if you are the mum or dad, brother or sister, partner or friend of a conservationist. It would be amazing to know that the people in my life could understand what I was going through when I came back from long trips away in remote areas, or while convincing local NGOs to employ me.

Before we continue

I do want to establish right from the start, that when I mention the word *'career'* throughout this book, I mean the time from first acting on a conservation passion, and with it all of the study, volunteering, and citizen science that may have been undertaken. As you may gather from my reasons for creating this community, paid jobs in conservation are surprisingly challenging to come by. So, if you are a conservationist reading this, let the word 'career' sum up your time and efforts so far in the industry.

Another term I want to establish right from the start is the word *'conservationist',* for when I say it, I mean anyone who is acting to conserve wildlife or ecosystems in their lives. If you're a stay-at-home mum and you try to minimise landfill waste around your household, then congratulations, you're a conservationist! If you are a lawyer who tries to reduce paper usage around the office, brings a keep cup to work every day, and encourages your office mates to improve their recycling efforts, then you guessed it- you are also a conservationist. Environmentalists, naturalists (*the kind who keep their clothes on...and those who don't too I guess*), biologists, zoologists, and ecologists alike all fall under this blanket term because I truly believe that anyone who can make strides to conserve our natural planet is indeed a conservationist.

I do need to stress that everyone who I have described, especially the mothers and lawyers out there, may not have experienced everything that I talk about in this book, as they may have never tried to pursue a career in the industry- but that's OK. The more people who take the time to listen to our stories, try to understand what we go through, and empathise with our cause, the better. I also want to acknowledge that the lived experiences that I touch on in this book are limited to the confines of my personal experience and those shared with me by members of my community. I understand that I will never know what it's like to personally defend one of the last remaining rhinos with a gun in my hand and my body on the line. Despite this, I do want to share as much information as I can within this book to help anyone from a mother who is reducing household waste, to a rhinoceros defender.

So now you know the context and the language of this book, you are now fully prepared to dive straight into the first chapter. I hope that you enjoy my meandering autobiographical journey into the life of a conservationist and that at least some of the content I touch on can help either a conservationist in your life or even yourself. Hopefully, by using this book as a guide, we can all conserve conservationists together.

| 2 |

The art of talking to a conservationist

Words have power

During the past decade or so that I have been working on conservation projects, I have never once consciously considered the language that others have used to talk to me or others in the field. Yet, on reflection, there have been countless moments where I have stewed for hours on end over the words that have been said to me during my time in the industry. Such throw-away words to others have been the cause of serious emotional responses from me which has often led me to feel irrational or overly emotional about my response. My feelings towards this experience changed when I noticed that words did seem to hold great power over conservationists as they spoke about their similar reactions in the stories they told, and I wanted to explore this more.

A common theme with people in the *Lonely Conservationists* community is that they are trudging through a largely underfunded industry, and no matter where they are in the world, conservationists are expected to volunteer beyond their capacity or need to constantly gain new skills. There are thousands of conservationists in the world right now who are working for free, for long periods in specialised positions that require extensive amounts of knowledge and skill. For this reason, their title holds a lot of weight as it is one of the only forms of value that they have to hold on to. Aside from their title, one of the most important factors contributing to the worth of a conservationist is how they are addressed and regarded in their professional circles.

So, what's next?

In the previous chapter, I introduced you to my lifelong mission to help conserve orangutan habitat and their future populations. Some people may read that story and think that I had an extremely rewarding life from the age of three to 24 years old, however, it's hard to imagine that people would hear that story and instantly understand the realities of my journey. The truth is that it wasn't until I was in North Sumatra, sitting alone on my bed in a house in the city, unable to get my permits to enter the forest, with builders peeping through my windows, that I took the time to look back and reflect on my journey. It was not until that moment that I appreciated the feat that I had gone through in dedicating my entire life to this one mission. I vividly remember the feeling of knowing that five-year-old Jessie would be so proud of me, and that equally so, 24-year-old Jessie was too. To put that into context, 19 years of my life were spent not appreciating the successes that I had achieved and rarely did I take time to dwell on wins. I was so focused on moving forward to achieve my goals that I never stopped to soak in the sunshine along the way. I now attribute the mentality of religiously focusing on moving forward to the frequently asked question: *what's next?*

I was interviewed for the *Nightlife* program on ABC radio about *Lonely Conservationists* when the very last question caught me by surprise. The host asked me what the future looked like for my community and what everyone could expect. I started by explaining how challenging it is to solve all of the issues that impact conservationists on my own, especially when this is a new path that has yet to be forged. I was promptly cut off and the interview ended before I could go on to say what projects I was working on. I sat with the discomfort of this question for some time and thought about how I was expected to wrap up my experiences of trying to navigate a systemic issue as just one person, in a tight bow. I tried to grapple with why I felt guilty about my response, even though the issue of conservationists being mistreated and underpaid isn't a simple issue to fix. To be honest, I didn't even know if this was an issue I could fix on my own.

I confronted this same question again weeks later after a Lonely Conservationist had sent me some questions that he wanted to ask me on his podcast, and there it was again. The very last question sitting there and haunting me.

What can we expect from *Lonely Conservationists* in the future?

As soon as I saw this question, I immediately hit reply on

the email to explain my discomfort with the implications of those words. It is important to understand how much pressure conservationists and environmentalists put on themselves to keep making strides to protect the species and landscapes they are so passionate about. I cannot stress enough how the self-imposed pressure to achieve perfection revels in the minds of most eco-conscious humans out there. We are often experiencing bouts of burnout, exhaustion and sometimes, are even nearing the cusp of apathy from how much we try to do to protect our planet as dedicated and resilient individuals. To ask what the future of our work entails suggests that the interviewer isn't content with how the project is now. It suggests, even indirectly or unintentionally, that what we are doing needs to be improved, changed, bigger or better.

Planting this seed in a conservationist's mind is fodder for insanity. Usually, we are already doing everything in our power to create change. Every change we do make only highlights the changes that we aren't making and that causes even more fear that we aren't doing enough. A simple question like, *"What can we expect from the future of your project?"*, can make us feel guilty, embarrassed, and inadequate for not having solved climate change, eliminated the microplastics in the ocean, or even prevented the unfair treatment of conservationists in our own lifetimes. This may seem like over the top or irrational thinking, as nobody blatantly made these accusations, but after bouts of exhaustion, this question could seem like a challenge.

A major issue I have with the conservation industry and

the media reporting of it is that monitoring is not seen as exciting or particularly sexy within the industry, yet is vital for measuring conservation success. This often leads to funding being directed at new and flashy projects, with old projects losing funding and not being able to be continued. Using media opportunities and funding to push organisations to continually start new projects instead of monitoring and maintaining existing efforts goes against the behaviour needed to achieve long-term sustainability. Having others repeatedly ask, *"What comes next?"* emphasises how un-important continuing old projects is, which perpetuates an unproductive cycle of starting new conservation projects that lose interest and funding over time. This abrupt ending of projects is always at the expense of the forgotten species, landscape or community that the project focuses on.

So now you may be wondering, if I shouldn't ask conservationists what their future looks like, what could I ask instead? A great alternative question could be to ask what they hope the future of their topic of study or work looks like, which takes the pressure off of the individual to feel as if they need to create this future alone. If somebody were to ask me what I hoped for in the future of conservationists, I would be inspired by imagining a world where individuals were valued for their work instead of daunted by the task of figuring out how I was going to achieve this vision on my own.

Growing, growing, gone

Growth is a great metric for success in many industries,

but financial or business growth isn't always the best indicator of success for conservationists. I remember sitting in a business incubator retreat that was created to help to develop environmentally-focused businesses. I thought for a while that *Lonely Conservationists* could be a business, but I found the incubator process overwhelming and constantly challenging my values. During the incubator, it was obvious that the notion of business success was the amount of money, staff and clients that were accumulated over time. I struggled with this application of success to *Lonely Conservationists* because my metrics of success sat more along the lines of individuals feeling valued for their work, and in turn, more long-term conservation efforts being actualised. On top of this, I had no idea how much my services or value was worth as I had never been properly funded for any of my conservation work. Imagine trying to assign a dollar figure to yourself when you have, in the past, been expected to give your services away for free or below minimum wage. Many conservationists struggle with assigning value to their services for this reason.

Following the pitch night for the incubator, I was invited to meet with the CEO of a development company who had been trying to increase sustainability efforts amongst their planning and decision making and was interested in how *Lonely Conservationists* could be involved in this process. He expressed how impressive it was for me to have gained such a substantial following so quickly and followed it up by asking how many community members I aspired to have. I responded that growth was not my intention for the community; rather, I aspired to provide the best services that I could to the people who were involved in the community. A smile spread across the CEO's face, and he expressed that he has also thought similarly, but has never found others who share his perspective. It was one of those rare moments where I felt understood by an industry superior.

For most people, achieving the most substantial conservation impact that we can means scaling down. This could mean focusing on reducing waste in our households rather than campaigning for our whole country or the world to reduce waste production. It could mean revegetating our properties with native plants and watching them house new species of wildlife, instead of rallying to protect the world's largest forests. For a lot of people, focusing on what we can do, tangibly, is a great remedy to the ever-persistent eco-anxiety.

This local mindset works really well around the world with communities focusing on conserving their natural habitats and native fauna. Bringing in international assistance leaves plenty of room for 'helicopter tourism', where foreigners drop in temporarily to assist, before leaving the rest of the work for the local people. This often causes more harm than good, as truly sustainable efforts, as I saw in my time in Indonesia, require cultural, behavioural and economic shifts. Employing oil palm workers to revegetate and care for the forest shifts the economic focus to conservation efforts and transforms the culture and community mindset from monoculture to permaculture. Involving the women in creating sustainable polybags and growing saplings in the nursery provides both an income and alternate career option for the women while simultaneously educating the children who accompany them and the wider village. No matter how long I stayed in these villages researching, living and working there, my use of resources and opportunities would always detract from the local community instead of adding to their livelihoods.

It is human nature to want everything to be bigger and better and to see that positive trajectory, but it is important to be mindful about the type of growth you are advocating for with conservationists, and empathise with their different metrics of growth success. Instead of the CEO of the development company asking me how many community members I'd like to accumulate, it would be great if he asked me the impact I'd like to have.

Let's talk money

When it comes to financial growth, I believe that this is a stigma that a lot of conservationists need to work on. It's almost as if conservationists are trained to repel money and feel severe guilt for prioritising an income. This training comes about from years of unpaid and minimum wage work as there are very few opportunities in early-career conservation that allow individuals to feel as if their work is worth the big bucks.

In a weird twist of events, I have found that advocating for myself in terms of payment has been a good indicator of who is going to value me, my time and my work. If a company or organisation is not willing to pay for my services, or at least offer a very nice wine and cheese basket, there is a good chance that they don't value my work and there is a high potential for disappointment. People pay for services that they need, want and value so it's a good way to catch the dangling carrots early by setting your price.

Setting a price for yourself is the next challenge, because, again, how do we know what we are worth if we have never had a business financially value us before? I have ecologist friends who have had to set their rates for contracting positions and have severely undervalued themselves, which isn't a fun feeling when all the other contractors are earning way more than them. I'd suggest looking at the industry rates online for your country to get a good starting point, and then assess your time, materials and workload against that. If you can, try to find others in the field to give you a ballpark figure, which is where having a community comes in handy.

A trick that I was taught in the business incubator that works well to calculate a full-time income, is to work out how much money you need to live comfortably and add the money that you need to achieve your saving goals to that. This is the figure that you need to earn to meet your personal objectives, so you can break down the monthly and weekly earnings from there that are necessary to maintain your lifestyle.

I believe that conservationists need to normalise building a sustainable life for ourselves, not just for the planet, and to do this, we need to get more comfortable talking about money. Don't be afraid to have conversations with your mentors and peers to find out how you can start valuing the work you do and allow others to value it too. You, my dear reader, are worth it.

A little empathy goes a long way

After I had spent the morning in Marapo Taman Negara, Malaysia, following elephant footprints to a place called *Gua Gajah* (elephant caves), I found myself in a literal depiction of a nightmare. After stepping one foot in the cave, I was instantly told to turn around and run, with the local guides running after us, ripping trees from the ground and carving them into spears with their machetes. My feet clad in the most practical footwear, reef shoes and waterproof socks, slowed me down as I sank into the mud while I ran. Echoing *ROARS* followed us until they didn't anymore and we could stop in a clearing, catch our breath and count our lucky stars.

That afternoon I returned to my hut and I messaged my family chat something to the extent of:

"I just ran for my life from a family of tigers".

My dad nonchalantly replied with something to the effect of *"That's nice, dear"* and proceeded to ask my brother how his football season had been going. I can't even believe I have to say this, but if your daughter doesn't eat breakfast, the most important meal of the day, and manages to outrun tigers in foot consuming clay- you best believe you should have some reassuring and loving words to say to her afterwards.

The reality of knowing conservationists is that you may hear these stories from us a lot. We outrun a tiger one day, the next it's an orangutan and then the next minute, your perception of the industry is that these life-or-death situations are just part and parcel of the job description.

To conservationists, however, there was a very real chance that we could have died or become seriously injured in each of the stories that we rattle off to you. Maybe as a self-protecting instinct, our friends and family often can't accept the realities of the stories we tell as instances that have happened to us. Maybe it's because they sound so fantastical- could they truly believe that I had spent my morning running from tigers? It seems very unlikely for a Wednesday morning, I will admit. The trick here is to not humour or trivialise these instances because no matter how outlandish these stories sound in the context of your own life, we are sharing with you a time that we almost got seriously injured or faced death. It would be like if I shared with my dad that I had a near-miss in a motorbike collision and he acted nonchalantly about it. It makes the conservationist feel as if their life is not important to the person on the other end of the story if the story is not received appropriately. Of course, my father would be extremely upset if anything were to happen to me, but, in that moment of having my tiger story pushed aside, it did not feel as if that were the case.

A blog by Gillian on the *Lonely Conservationists* website details other serious impacts of trivialising serious recounts of dangerous situations in the field:

When I would return home from some extra long field days covered in mud and blood, I secretly relished the horrified looks I got from housemates and would often joke about the times I almost got heat stroke during long hikes or broken bones from sliding down some steep terrain. Online, I saw other biologists proudly sharing their similar field horror stories and the unbelievable stress they were under in school or work, and felt validated. People praised me for working so hard and putting myself out there, feeding the beast within that associated being reckless with working hard.

Gillian's story goes on to describe how she was fuelled by these interactions to fetch a camera trap from her field site in unsafe weather conditions:

After I reached the camera, I was soaked to the bone, and my teeth began to chatter uncontrollably. That was when my brain started getting increasingly foggy. My legs grew heavy as I stumbled back down the trail and I lost feeling in my tongue. I began to mutter nonsensically to myself as I just kept trying (and failing) to put one foot in front of the other. At one point I sat cross-legged in the mud for a few minutes, trying to summon some energy to get back to the parking lot. For some reason, the most frightening part of it all was the strange, deep longing I felt to crawl off the trail and curl up in a hollowed-out redwood tree to sleep. It was all I could think about.

Somehow, despite a glitchy GPS, no phone service, and my

brain shutting down from what I assume was some level of hypothermia, I finished the long trek back to the parking lot and then drove an hour home in the dark. How I managed that, I have no idea- I was not in any condition to drive, but at that point my brain had turned off. I was shaking violently (the truck's heating was broken) and only remember flashes of it to this day. After taking an hour-long warm shower and sleeping for most of the next three days, I finally had a clear head again and realized just how much I messed up. My insecurity had put me in danger and I vowed it would never happen again. It took a lot of time and self-reflection to work past the anxiety I would feel when hiking alone after that day.

Romanticising, humouring or trivialising what we go through in the field is often used as a coping mechanism for us conservationists, so it's important for others not to play into that. As you can see, Gillian was compelled to put herself in an unsafe situation where she may not have made it home because of the way both conservationists and their friends and family treat near-death experiences as either trivial or a badge of honour. Instead of dismissing a conservationist's dangerous story or egging them on to share more with pride, consider the impact that your reaction and subsequent words have. It's important that you become a safe space to confide in, instead of the cause of another dangerous incident.

Who is a conservationist anyway?

An easy way to validate a conservationist is to not invalidate their worth by questioning their status within the industry. If someone you know is proudly putting 'conservationist' as their title, let them have it. Everyone who is making strides to conserve our natural world is making some kind of difference, no matter how small, and therefore, they are a conservationist. Scientists have enough trouble acknowledging their value through titles already and so it can be extremely soul-crushing to have a friend or family question your conservationist identity, especially if you have trained in another field before moving into the industry. Even after completing an honours degree in ecology and working on multiple ecological field studies, I still sit uncomfortably with my personal Instagram URL being a play on the word 'ecologist'. Despite the degrees, work, or experience someone has in a field, it is hard to own a title if they aren't getting paid and don't have a business card with their title under their name to reaffirm their position.

Natasha echoes this sentiment in her story on *Lonely Conservationists:*

> *I even second-guessed myself when I had to put a label on my Instagram account. Can I call myself a scientist? Officially? Yes. I've done everything a field biologist does, just as a volunteer. I am a field biologist. I am a researcher. And I am a conservationist. Most importantly, I am also myself.*

Running a webinar series called *Lonely Conversationists*, I was able to hear the perspectives of conservationists who had come into the industry from other backgrounds. The two speakers shared their impostor syndrome regarding their validity in the conservation space, having trained in other fields and only recently allowing themselves to explore their passion for nature. This impostor syndrome was partially self-imposed but also enforced by other conservationists questioning them about their skills, expertise and experience. Gate-keeping brings absolutely nothing positive to the industry and if a conservationist's dream is to grow and foster a greener world, I don't understand why all conservationists can't rejoice in other's efforts in contributing to making it happen. The more the merrier, I say!

Seeking help

If you are a psychologist and a conservationist comes into your office and sits down on that slinky chair of yours to regale you with the struggles that they have been experiencing in the industry, it is important not to suggest that they should switch careers. The truth is, a conservationist's passion is blood deep which often causes environmentally-minded individuals to withstand much more than they otherwise would to fulfil their environmental dreams. I have had friends suffering from bad bouts of post-traumatic stress disorder (PTSD), depression and anxiety whose problems, on the surface, could seem to be resolved by a career change. Even my husband, Todd, gave me an intervention just before

I created *Lonely Conservationist*s and told me that if I didn't have a job in conservation that supported me financially by the time I was 30, then it would be time to find a new career path.

Now, it is important to note that Todd's reasons for this ultimatum were not income-based, but rather, he was just tired of seeing me go through the same struggles over and over again. I imagine it must be challenging to see someone you love not being valued for the hours of work that you see them invest and witness their self-belief deplete every time a dangling-carrot-style opportunity ultimately never delivers on the carrot. As it was never an option for me to not be a conservationist, I had to get creative to work out how I could sustain a life for myself within the industry. I believe a five-year time frame to reassess my tactics was more appropriate than telling me to give up on my dreams, and as someone who now has the most established career path of my life, I am grateful for Todd's concern and reasonable boundary setting for my career. At the time of writing this, I will be 30 next year, and I believe I have done enough to warrant Todd's belief in my future as a conservationist.

If you are a psychologist, family member or friend reading this, it would be great if you could instead help to remind conservationists that they are people. I know that it seems weird to have to say this, but we often get so caught up in being conservationists that we forget to just be ourselves, whether we be the family member, the friend, the sportsperson, artist or foodie that we are outside of the industry. Sometimes, we invest so much of our self-worth in our title, our work or our environmental contributions that we forget that we have worth as we are.

I would like to suggest to conservationists that you try to find some people who you can talk to who understands your conservation experience, not as a replacement for medical advice, but as a refuge from feeling misunderstood amongst your wider social circles. I would also like to suggest to the wider social circles that you take the time to listen to your conservationist friend or family and understand and sympathise with the stress that they may be under. I had a friend message me after listening to the *How To Conserve Conservationists Podcast* that Todd and I released, following the publication of the first edition of this book. The message stated that my friend was always jealous of my passion, so she never considered that I may be encumbered by financial strain or the other frustrations brought on by working in the environmental sector. Sometimes it's important for us as conservationists to be honest with the people in our lives, so that they can understand how to understand us better as individuals and accommodate us where we need them to.

Take this message home

As we have seen from this chapter, language can play a huge role in the life of a conservationist, from their career success to avoiding danger and seeking comfort. If you ever see a conservationist in the wild sipping a drink and looking out at the sunset, or on a couch reading a fantasy novel or even playing hopscotch in the yard, please use your language to reinforce how amazing it is that they are looking after themselves and for just being a person. This is something we often forget, that resting and relaxing is important for healthy cell division, mood and overall health and wellbeing. If we are constantly burnt out, no mouse, moose or musk ox will benefit from our work. If a conservationist comes to talk to you remember to empathise, take them seriously, and listen. Sometimes, no words are needed; just a snack and a hug will do.

| 3 |

We are all impostors

You're a good scientist

In the first year that *Lonely Conservationists* existed in the world, we accumulated 50 blogs that were shared on the website, 49 of them sitting alongside mine. After first sharing my story as a plea to finally determine whether or not I was the loneliest conservationist in the world, I ended the year with a huge community of thousands of conservationists who had been vulnerable and brave enough to speak up beside me. These conservationists spanned the globe, generations and cultures. As the year ended, people continued to share their experiences with the community and even to this day, stories by lonely conservationists are still being published once a week.

The scientist within me couldn't help but notice the incredible data set that lay before me. After the first 70 blogs, I decided to look deeper into these stories and find solutions to help lonely conservationists from recommendations that they didn't even know they were writing. Through my time exploring the scope of *Lonely Conservationists*, I came across three women who were also researching constraints to conservationists. One of them researched gender equality in conservation workplaces, another looked into the implications of failure and the third scientist researched resilience and capacity building. As someone who had spent a year witnessing the incredible benefits of community, I introduced them all and we started to meet regularly to chat about our work and discuss possible ways to collate our findings and collaborate on projects.

Instantly the dynamic of these three insanely wonderful women who were completing PhDs and affiliated with universities contrasted to my position outside of academia. I was nervous at first to be different, as many academics have dismissed me in the past for not being affiliated with a university, but over time, I learnt to own my space as an independent, and acknowledge the value of the views and experiences that I bring to the table. I am still, to this day, so thankful that everything I add to the conversation is well received and considered important input. It made my day when one of the women said *"That's an excellent point"* or *"You're a really good scientist for thinking that"*. This praise means so much because *Lonely Conservationists* and the wider scientific community are rife with impostor syndrome.

Making a name for myself

Impostor syndrome is the experience of feeling like a fraud in whatever you are doing. It is so prevalent in science because of the elitism and pressure to constantly publish scientific papers and accumulate citations. When I was studying for my honours degree, my supervisor told me that I could never get anywhere or do anything without using his name. After this, he continued to restrict my opportunities and push me down throughout my entire degree to assert his dominance and boost his prestige higher. As a strong confident woman who *snaps fingers* don't need no man, I worked hard to establish myself in North Sumatra and make my name to be known by and build my own professional network. Because of my dedication to this cause, I ended up winning an award for my research and speaking at multiple conferences and festivals. As punishment for this, my supervisor denied me the right to a moderation meeting at the end of my degree which is a compulsory and standard component for all students completing an honours degree across Australia. There is no question as to why people continue to feel unworthy in science, even when their research has incredible implications for the future of our society and environment.

Even within a safe community of like-minded individuals, conservationists in my community still consistently show signs of impostor syndrome during communication. When asked to share their story on the website after getting to know them, the most common response that I get from lonely conservationists is that they are "Only a student", "Only a volunteer" or "Only early on in their careers". I find it so interesting that we have been taught to believe that insight from these demographics isn't important when, in reality, they are extremely important perspectives to consider to understand the wider constraints within the industry. It astounds me that members of my community don't believe they are worthy enough to talk about the times they have failed, lessons they have learnt and hurdles they have overcome. They don't believe their voice is worthy, they don't believe it has value or that it matters. I never imagined that impostor syndrome could reach this far into the psyche of conservationists and that despite being so early in their careers, their voice has already been taken away from them.

This is why there is such a weight to the validation that these women give me for my ideas and research. This is why their praise is not just an offhand comment that lasts a second in time, but rather notions I still carry with me in everything I do. It is important to remind conservationists of the role they have to play in this world and the value of their voice. In my small community of women looking at conservationists, my value is that I am outside of academia and can see what is happening in a community of globally distributed individuals. There is value to my differences and there is an important story that can be told by the people in my community. My voice matters and equally so do the voices of all other conservationists.

Taking a closer look

When I looked at a subset of 70 blogs that my community had submitted, one element of my focus was looking at the emotional language that the authors had used. Interestingly, the most commonly used emotive word that kept cropping up in all of the blogs was 'love'. Conservationists in my community were not shy in expressing their love for plants, for animals, for nature and all of the people in their lives, both inspirational and alongside them on their journeys. It is no surprise that conservationists love what they do, and love who they do it for as they are not driven by a high income or a nice office in a tall building in the city. Conservationists are driven by love.

Looking at the next most frequent emotive terms, it was sadness and hardship that equally followed love. To me, this finding represents the conflict that conservationists face in loving conservation work, loving wildlife and loving nature, but feeling impacted by the conditions in which they are expected to undertake this work. Oftentimes, conservationists face challenges in finding work and upon finding work, experience challenging conditions throughout the job duration.

Often, this dichotomy is severe, where the good aspects of the industry are life-changing, beautiful and once-in-a-lifetime moments where you find yourself in new places, uncovering new findings and helping to work on meaningful projects. In contrast, the not-so-good elements may be soul-destroying as you may not be able to support yourself, be living in remote or harsh environmental conditions or receive a lack of workplace support due to small, underfunded organisations being so prevalent in the industry. Oftentimes, taking a job in the industry is fraught with compromise. I have worked in beautiful locations across the globe but have spent my savings to do so. I have landed a great job title and have earned enough money to live on doing work I am passionate about, but I couldn't sleep at night due to anxiety caused by workplace bullying. I have lived my five-year-old dreams of working in orangutan conservation, only to realise that I could not sustainably contribute to the inter-generational behaviour change needed for the long-term conservation that is rooted in local culture.

Conservationist or cheap labour?

The love we have for what we do lends itself to exploitation throughout our whole careers and this has to be acknowledged. Organisations know that we will work for free or even pay to work because we love the work that we do. Workplaces can get away with not treating their employees fairly because they can use one of the thousands of job-seeking conservationists to take the place of any employees that leave. Unfortunately for us, conservationists are eager to bend over backwards to do whatever it takes to obtain and keep a job, even at their own expense.

We are told, as students, that we will never land ourselves a job in the industry unless we have volunteer experience, but how much are we expected to endure? I have volunteered for over a decade across different countries, Australian states and fields of research. It got to the point where my dad had to sit me down and declare that I had more than enough experience and that the next role I have should be a paid one. That seems like a reasonable request, as you never see a bricklayer spending a decade laying bricks for free before he starts getting paid to build houses.

In the world of conservation, however, it is not that simple.

I once had a man tell me how confident he was in the future of the job market for conservationists and that over the coming years, he predicted that people across all professions will wish that they had some sort of conservation training. I asked him how that could be possible as there are so many people in my community with years of training, and no jobs in sight for a large percentage of them. The need for conservation efforts has always been necessary, but government funding to enable conservation projects to go ahead is often very thin on the ground. An underfunded conservationist lifestyle is not easy to upkeep and it is only accessible to those privileged enough to have access to other means of support. Some incredibly talented people cannot sustain a conservation career because they have to find work that financially supports themselves and their families. This huge limitation to access restricts a range of demographics from following their conservation dreams and removes many valuable contributions to the field.

It is understandable that this man would have missed the reality of a life in conservation that many of us experience, considering he had only ever been exposed to accessible opportunities and positive conversations. Perceptions of the industry such as his, are a key driver as to why I believe that it's important to start and continue conversations about the broader experience of being a conservationist.

What do you do?

It is no surprise that conservationists don't feel valued for their work when everyone else in society is getting rewarded for their efforts with a paycheck at the end of the week. Conservationists have to keep looking back to their love and passion for a sense of validation and remind themselves of the rewarding work they do as they stare into the disappointing void which is their bank account. This is also exacerbated by the pressure from friends and family to get a *"real job"*. If you don't earn an income and don't have a job title, it is hard to answer the commonly asked question of *"What do you do?"* without the urge to justify your whole life's decisions. Even if you do say *"I'm a conservationist"*, there are bound to be prying questions about the scope and capacity of your work. Not to mention the embarrassment of being asked if your job pays well and having to admit you work for free or pay for the privilege.

I vividly remember the time when I had just started *Lonely Conservationists* and it was really taking off. I had taken the wrong train home *(classic Jessie)* and so decided to catch an Uber for the last 10 minutes instead of spending another two hours rerouting my train travels. I sat in the passenger seat hoping that the driver wouldn't ask me what I did. I had just been in the city for a meeting with a professional from a renowned Australian organisation and so I was dressed appropriately. Despite this, I couldn't explain why I was just in a professional meeting because I wasn't working a job, but rather, I was running an organisation that I had created and wasn't earning a living from. When he inevitably asked, I felt like I had to explain my life story to him and justify my decisions as to why I was living outside of the societal norm.

I wished I had a one-word answer to give, like '*doctor*' or '*lawyer*', words that are so simple to convey, but alas! I found myself trying to explain the perils of being a conservationist. The driver probably didn't care and was just making small talk, but for me, the situation was the cause of existential dread.

Scientists vs internet experts

Another phenomenon that amplifies our impostor syndrome is the Dunning-Kruger Effect. This effect describes the many people who reside in the comment sections online, who know a little bit about something and therefore consider themselves to be experts. The effect also encompasses very knowledgeable scientists who don't think they know much at all because they are aware of how much more there is to know and how very little they actually know in the scheme of things. This effect contrasts a perceived ability, like the online commenters have, with an actual ability like the impostor syndrome-riddled scientists. This false perception of intelligence can make knowledgeable people doubt their knowledge and in turn, validate the perceived knowledge of people who only know a little bit. This phenomenon can leave us questioning our true credentials and value in society when really, we probably have more knowledge and experience than necessary to confidently speak up in public forums.

I have been grappling with this phenomenon a lot as an educator. I thought that to teach, I must have to be an expert on whatever I am teaching about. In some ways, this is true, as I couldn't teach a class on carpentry because I have no training in the field. But there is no way that a carpenter would have to teach me their full scope of knowledge to teach me how to build a basic table. Similarly, I realise that the entire sum of my knowledge isn't important when teaching students, parents or teachers about the environment because, in the confines of the education program, what I teach must be simple, digestible and applicable. Sometimes, it's important to remember that a vast brain full of knowledge isn't entirely necessary to be good at a conservation-based job.

Touching base with reality

As you can see, surviving the ominous loom of impostor syndrome is nearly impossible for a conservationist. From the elitism of academia to not being financially valued for our work and questioning our roles in society, the feelings of not being worthy are hard to escape. It is important to note, however, that we don't have to feel like impostors forever. After identifying what is impostor syndrome and what we need to improve on in ourselves, we can then start to adjust our ways of thinking about our lives and start to rid the notion of being an impostor from our brains.

When I was in North Sumatra for my honours, I could see that I was not the sum of my supervisor's actions or opinions as there were other indicators that my work had value. Like the award I won and the scientists who were interested in speaking to me about my work or even wanting to collaborate. Although his actions towards me lingered in my psyche for years, I could escape those feelings of not being worthy by continuing to focus on the positive feedback I had received from others- even if this did take some time. Even now, I can proudly say that I am a *'conservationist conservationist'* or a sustainability educator without needing to share my whole life story. Despite the fluctuations in my income, I have come to believe in the value and importance of my work, no matter if it's paid, for an organisation or for myself. Constantly having to justify a place for yourself in society is exhausting, so it's important to carve a space for yourself that you are content with, no matter what others think.

Take this message home

If you see a conservationist in the wild, it is important to remind them that they don't need to justify who they are. They have intrinsic value whether they are a student, early in their career, volunteering or partaking in citizen science. If they are a parent who has started making environmental changes to their family household, the minister for the environment or anyone in between, what they do for our planet has value. Nobody deserves to feel like a fraud for doing what they love and it is important for the future of young conservationists that they feel empowered to use their voice and make the change they want to see in the world. Those voices and those changes - that's right - they have value.

| 4 |

Take the "u" out of failure

High risk, low reward

Conservationists are notoriously afraid of failure and this is mostly because the stakes are too high and the culture is often too unforgiving in our workplaces. As a ridiculously under-funded industry, our projects and businesses, as a whole, often rely on sparsely given grant money and donations from kind believers in our work. Because of this, conservationists are often terrified of *"wasting"* the money we do get, in hopes that if we use the funds correctly, we will continue to get more money to sustain the longevity of our work. Subsequently, wildlife rehabilitation programs often experience extremely high rates of failure in the first release with many animals dying from a multitude of reasons that depend on the field site and species. For this reason, I have experienced wildlife rehabilitation programs that never release or miss the prime release time for the wildlife they keep, in fear of killing all of their beloved animals after weeks, months, or even years of caring for them.

Toxic work culture

Possibly as a result of high risk, low resource work environments, I have also experienced a high rate of toxic workplace cultures spanning locations and conservation focus throughout the industry. It is impossible to embrace failure yourself as an employee when your management demands perfectionism and frankly on occasion, impossibly met standards.

There was one instance when I was working for a conservation organisation that facilitated fortnightly trips to a local forest to weed invasive species and plant trees nearby. As the volunteers were usually regular attendees, the staff arranged to take them out on a picnic for a special celebration in a different location at the end of the year. As I was feeling extremely ill, to the point of being bedridden, I let my boss know a week in advance that I would not be able to help staff this event. She arranged to cover me herself at the event but also made me come into work during the week when I was still bedridden, to do all the food shopping for the picnic. She acted like I didn't have a choice to do this task if I wanted to keep my job, so I went despite feeling, and looking, like death.

The event came and went and once restored to good health, I returned to work. Feeling like something was amiss, I noticed my co-worker didn't show up for work that day and the whole atmosphere felt very different in the office. My boss cornered me when nobody was around and proceeded to yell at me as if I was a naughty child. She blamed me for making her do extra work by attending the event, when she already had thousands of other things to do, even though it was previously arranged that she would cover my spot. She also told me that I had provided the guests with the wrong address, as the location they were meeting at had an incorrect address on Google when I had looked it up. I was extremely new to the state and the location they were meeting at and so I had no idea that the advertised address would be incorrect. Fortunately, the only person impacted by this mistake was a member of staff and not any of the volunteers, but this still wasn't seen as even remotely relieving for my boss. After apologising and suggesting ways that I could mitigate these issues into the future, she continued to yell at me for not taking responsibility for my actions in the past. Since that incident, I could no longer sleep at night in fear of being left alone with my boss at work and being unjustly berated again. I eventually had to leave that workplace for good to conserve my sanity.

They don't want you to succeed

As you can imagine, I didn't just leave that job because of how I was treated for one single mistake, as it takes a fair bit to break down a conservationist who has secured themselves a job. Conservationists aren't people who let go of job roles lightly. As well as not being failure-positive, the culture of that workplace wasn't even success-positive. On one occasion, my boss told me excitedly that she appeared in a magazine that week, to which I excitedly exclaimed, "*Me too!*" as we both held up our magazine segments. In a moment perfect for a hi-five or appropriate celebratory gesture, my boss promptly glared at me, turned away and didn't speak to me again for the rest of the week. It is important in any job that the staff feel empowered to be the best versions of themselves and to grow and evolve with the support of superiors. Sadly, with such "disposable" conservationists in such an over-populated industry, having a good work culture is just not a priority for many managers.

Other conservationists in my community have also experienced this type of management in the workplace. Lisa details her experience:

> Instead of working on papers, probing for nests, doing necropsies, or even interacting on the social media page, I was given a list of chores every day. I went into the giant dumpster and recycling bin to move garbage around. I cleaned the toilets. I sanitized the necropsy lab. I washed cars and UTVs for people who were in the field. I filled up people's gas. I cleaned our office kitchen. I broke my back moving ice chests for people camping. I reorganized and took inventory of every single closet on their property. I became the person assigned all of the office chores while co-workers were spending time camping, doing GIS work, or on the organization's social media pages. Even co-workers hired to a lower position than I did not have half of the janitorial duties I did.
>
> I took matters into my own hands multiple times and inquired about different projects I could work on. Every time I asked for an assignment, I was told to sweep. Every time I asked to edit a paper, I was told to empty the dehumidifier. I was feel-

ing frustrated but kept telling myself that this was a part of being in conservation.

Until one day, I finally got picked to help design a logo for our department. I looked forward to it every day. I was excited to be working so closely with the head of our department and my personal hero, Ashley. I thought this would be my chance to prove my worth above my cleaning skills and get recognized. I had dozens of designs to choose from. I even got my friend, a professional artist, to draw us a sea turtle for free to use. I worked on them in my free time just hoping to contribute to the legacy of the organisation I was serving under. Ashley eventually stopped answering me, or even acknowledging me in the office. This stung colder than usual because not only had she been my personal hero for years but my desk was directly outside of her office. I also learnt that later on, she did not know my name. She didn't know I was the person she was emailing. I was one out of five people who worked in the office.

Unfortunately, these experiences are prolific within the conservation industry. Young and vibrant individuals are excited to be hired to work for a conservation project that they can feel will be a great career progression opportunity and a fulfilling experience relevant to their passions. The personalities and promises that are present in management during the interview stage can appear as a façade and casually slip away as the job starts and the cheap labour begins. Conservationists often endure completing tasks unrelated to the job that they signed up for, in hopes that eventually, these tasks will lead them to the jobs that they did sign up for. Inevitably, giving your all to these types of workplaces often ends in disappointment rather than success. If your mental and physical health is being impacted by your place of work, it is better to find another job that will value you, your time and your skills.

It is important to mention here that if you are uncertain about leaving a toxic workplace, you must remember that you do not owe them anything. Your health and wellbeing are far more important than the running of that workplace or the perception of your superiors.

I experienced this exact phenomenon at a job in New South Wales years before I worked for the boss that I mentioned at the start of this chapter. At the time, I presumed that the misrepresentation of the job role and toxic work environment was an isolated incident and not a commonality in the industry. I hadn't yet grasped the consequences of working for small family-owned businesses that lack a human resources department or union. These kinds of businesses are common throughout the industry and trap staff in a dangerous predicament when dealing with conflict as there are often no higher-ups to turn to if there is a disagreement with your direct management.

In this particular job, I was hired to consult for tourism companies to help them reduce their energy costs and put that money towards local wildlife conservation. What ended up happening was that I became the in-house hotel administration officer and babysitter as the owners jetted off to France for a holiday and left me to take over their business and children. There were dangling carrot opportunities thrown around, suggesting that I may be able to work with the owner in Dubai and get deep into the conservation work if I pushed through. Inevitably, I was punished for being sick, apparently a common theme in my career, as well as for many other irrational reasons. One of these irrational reasons included being yelled at on the drive home from picking the owners up from the airport after their holiday, despite them not having arrived at the property yet to see the work I had done. This was the first time I walked out on a job because I couldn't mentally sustain the role.

How is this viable?

To this day, I am unsure why failure is treated so negatively in many of the workplaces that I and many others have worked in. This negative reinforcement to simple mistakes results in curating negative relationships between staff and their management. Not only this, but a toxic culture can also invoke worse work outputs from the staff by creating a stressful environment where they are too scared to ask questions or clarify uncertainties.

It is bewildering to me that it seems more cost-and-time-effective to continually retrain new staff, instead of curating a good work environment and a healthy cohort of long-term and dedicated staff members. From my perspective, it is a no-brainer that a long-term and healthy staff cohort would be more reliable, could alleviate the workload of management due to less training or micromanaging requirements, and would contribute to long-term relationships with clients and conservation outputs. A healthy work culture would no doubt lead to a more economically viable and less stressful workplace, which would reflect positively on growth and the outward reputation of the company. Especially when conservation circles are so tight-knit, it isn't wise to have people out in the community who won't advocate for a workplace. Even if a reputation seems good due to ex-staff being afraid to speak out, there will still be the talk amongst potential staff members, former staff members, and people who have heard stories about the business or organisation through the grapevine.

Another point to consider is that it must be truly taxing for these people and their businesses to create failures out of incidents that don't have the pre-requisites to be failures. Being sick isn't a failure, especially when communicated effectively with management before any tasks are due if time off is needed. Small mistakes and unforeseen circumstances can be moved past with ease if they are acknowledged, accounted for and moved on from. In both of the jobs I mentioned, these businesses lost a staff member due to what would be classified as a total non-issue in many other workplaces. This is also true for Lisa and her former employer.

The biggest failure associated with these businesses is that they don't foresee the disappointment that inevitably occurs when a staff member finds out that they are not being employed to do the job that they originally signed up for, in worse conditions than they could ever imagine.

The benefits of failing

I have come to understand the risks of discussing failure in conservation roles, as there may be risks of losing the minimal funding and resources that a company has if it can't prove that its efforts are working. In a highly competitive field, it is not preferable to highlight your shortcomings when there are so many other competing organisations that may swipe your next funding opportunity. There is also the factor that releasing information about a high percentage of wildlife release deaths may appear to donors and public supporters that the organisation is involved in harming more animals than they protect. Being honest about survival rates following a release could even be portrayed as wasting resources by investing in care for animals that will most likely not make it. As we have discussed in more detail, staff may be afraid to discuss failures with management in fear of being reprimanded.

This is problematic because the opportunities for organisations to learn from each other are few and far between if failures aren't discussed openly. This secrecy can lead to organisations making the mistakes of others without any warning or education. In an industry with so few resources and a shared goal to protect wildlife and natural spaces, it would be useful for organisations to share their failures so that others don't have to put more wildlife and habitat at risk by repeating the same mistakes. Imagine if a vervet monkey organisation, for instance, shared the details of their releases with other monkey conservation organisations in Africa so that they could collaborate and consolidate information and share what worked and what didn't. This could provide better opportunities for release success than are currently available in a competitive network of organisations.

I'd love to see a world where conservation conferences encouraged the discussion of failures so that each mass get-together amongst similar projects would result in more learning outcomes and higher future success rates for organisations. If communicating failures was more normalised in the industry, it would also allow donors to be better judges when allocating their money, as they could see who is learning from past mistakes and who is using the money to maintain ongoing un-successful projects.

I'd also love to see staff and management have an open dialogue about errors in their work and company shortcomings. If failures became opportunities to grow, learn and improve, in terms of both staff skills and company practices, how amazing would the growth and success of conservation organisations become!

Put it on the wall

In a panel I spoke on, titled *'Never Waste a Good Failure: What You Can Do To Fail Intelligently And Why It Matters'*, I learnt about the concept of a *'Failure Wall'*. My ears perked up the second I heard the term and I was so astonished to hear that some amazing leaders out there have walls in their offices that are dedicated to showcasing the failures of their staff. I was so inspired by this concept that I made a virtual failure wall for my community that they can access through the website. Showcasing failures is a great method of normalising failures as a human experience, but also highlighting the ways that we have grown and learnt from them. It has been incredible to see management level staff contribute to my failure wall, allowing early-career conservationists to see that no matter how far you advance through your career, there are still mistakes to be made. Since creating the failure wall, I heard Julia Migné, director of Conservation Optimism, mention it during an interview and I was, and still am, so glad that it has been noticed and positively regarded amongst the community.

You are not a failure for something you can't control

Interestingly, during conversations with my community, I've realised they are extremely harsh on themselves when it comes to defining failures, to the point where they see failure as something that happens independently to consequences of their behaviour. Many lonely conservationists have shared with me that they had failed because their jobs and internships were cancelled due to the COVID-19 global pandemic. They had also claimed to have failed when they didn't get accepted into a job position with a high number of candidates, with one person even saying that they failed for coming in second for a new position.

As an opposite experience, during the failure panel, we had to share a time that we had failed with a small group and practice sharing our stories in a constructive way. After hearing each other's stories, the members of the group had to practice constructively listening, commenting, and asking useful questions. This was a very challenging experience for me to come up with a single failure, as every time I had perceived myself to fail, I had felt it was a reflection of someone's perception of me and not a direct reflection on my actions. The other times in my life that hadn't gone to plan had resulted in great learning or pivoting opportunities that aided me somewhere else down the line.

I ended up thinking back in time to my undergraduate degree where I was tasked with debating in a team with the position that we were for cloning animals. I was so passionately against cloning animals that a documentary on bringing back the Tasmanian tiger, or Thylacine, was enough to anger me into creating a petition that decreased sales of a national sandwich franchise overnight.

I know what you're wondering and you're right: Thylacines don't have anything to do with sandwiches. The notion of spending millions of dollars on bringing back a non-viable species instead of investing that money into the preservation of critically endangered animals made me inspired to act on a cause I was passionate about, which was palm oil. Don't worry, I will divulge further into this story a bit later on.

Because of my strong aversion to the topic, I physically couldn't bring myself to take the debate seriously or even formulate a proper argument for cloning, to the detriment of my teammate's grades. One of my teammates was furious with me afterwards, which made me realise that I should have shown empathy to their involvement in the project, instead of being so headfast in my views and beliefs. Since that day,

I have made sure to put my own values aside in times where they may be directly detrimental to others around me.

I believe that conservationists should be more realistic about whether a failure is an action that we could have prevented or something completely outside of our control. It seems as if many conservationists are harbouring self-criticism and doubt about events that were well beyond their intervention. I can understand why they have these beliefs, as the perception of how conservationists have failed may have been warped by toxic superiors over time. Thankfully for me, there have been times where I could tell that my bosses were not a fan of me as a person and that their actions did not necessarily reflect my true abilities.

On one occasion, the boss from my community-organising role was talking with a volunteer about analysing the data that her field staff had collected on koalas. As a medical doctor and professor, the volunteer explained to her that I have had more experience analysing these types of data sets and that she should work with me to produce this science. Without even looking at me once, she then proceeded to question if she even needed science at all, obviously irritated that he should suggest me as a knowledgeable source. Without hesitation, I explained that data is a great way of proving to funding sources that your efforts are having the conservation impacts that you claim they are having. I went on to say that producing data is also a great way to showcase that the conservation efforts you are working on are as important and as necessary for the populations of koalas as you say they are. The volunteer enthusiastically agreed, and so my boss abruptly ended the conversation and drove me back to the office. This moment was key in assuring me that I had good ideas and that I knew what I was doing in the scientific community, but my boss had other agendas and was acting unprofessionally. Without the reassurance from this respected volunteer and scientist, I may have believed that I was the sum of all the failures that my boss perceived me to be.

Just perfect

I have been thinking a lot about perfectionism and how it's so prolific in our society. To be honest with you, I must admit that I have never suffered from perfectionism in my work. I was the kid that completed my assignments the day I got them just to get them out of the way- and yes, I know, you have never heard of a kid like that before. I tended to rush my work because I felt like my life was a race between growing up and species hurtling toward extinction. I found that it was easier to *"just do things"* and learn from my mistakes rather than agonise about how immaculate my work was. As proof that I still do this, I quickly published the first edition of this book to say what I needed to say, and then after reflecting on my words, I am here again to add changes and improvements. This is why it is so challenging for me to work for individuals who demand perfection. I am a person who likes to fail fast and learn, rather than agonise over something long term and hope that it's right the first time. Riding a bike, learning to write, and most tasks that we learnt as children, took time to practice and evolve. It seems unrealistic to expect perfection from people when we are used to working in stages to gradually improve over time.

My rush to conserve species that I perceived to be hurtling toward extinction was also coupled with my perception, as a child and teenager, that I was the only one vaguely interested in protecting wildlife. This false perception ultimately led to me feeling personally responsible for fixing many of the world's problems. Of course, in doing my degree, getting into the industry and, now being a part of *Lonely Conservationists,* what gives me hope is that there are so many passionate people out there who are interested in conserving the smallest nematodes in the soil, to the largest whales in the ocean. If we don't have a realistic perception of the other conservationists like us in the world, it may feel as if a lot of the world's problems can fall on our shoulders, which is a lot of pressure for individuals to carry alone.

I remember being an angsty 15-year-old, sitting on a swing set alone in a park because my best friend, and then crush, told me that I could never have any positive impact on our planet. What a surreal experience that just short of a decade later, I ran into him at a pub where he proceeded to brag to the person he was with, saying that he was responsible for all my successes by challenging me to prove him wrong. It's a *'You're damned if you do, damned if you don't'* situation where, if you don't have a positive impact on our planet, you fail, but if you do make a notable change, someone else will swoop in there and take ownership of your efforts. This happened to me a second time when an article was published about the decrease in sandwich sales due to my palm oil petition. In the comments of the article, people who had previously made me feel isolated for my values left comments taking credit for my successful movement. Sometimes it feels as if nobody cares about helping me succeed, but everyone wants to be there to take a slice of success when I have it.

In conservation, success isn't always easy to come by with such large odds stacked against us. Throughout my life, I wish that I had more help, guidance, and support through my battles and fewer people trying to claim my small wins as their own.

There is one moment in my life that I will never forget. I got a call from the head office of the national sandwich franchise saying that the head honcho had seen the impact that I had on their sales with my petition. They warned me that they were coming to pull me out of my GIS lecture and take me to their head office to meet with the CEO of the company. I was shitting myself because the plot twist is that I actually worked for the sandwich franchise at the time and there was a concern that I would lose my job and fail my exams due to missing this lecture. I called my dad, as I always do in tricky situations, and he said the following words to me that I will never forget.

> *"Jessie, you have been fighting for orangutans your whole life and this is your chance to make a real impact. You have a choice to back down and take the safe option, or you can fight the fight you have always wanted to."*

Those words made me realise for the first time that actually making a difference wouldn't be easy or risk-free or even necessarily fun, but it was something that was within my reach if I could muster the courage. With the strength of my dad's support, I got in the company car that day and drove to the office with a woman who I had sometimes seen around work. When we got there, I sat around the conference call speaker alongside the other HR representatives and I talked to the CEO of the Australian sandwich franchise. I negotiated with them, asked the hard questions and, on top of all of the chaos, somehow managed to keep my job.

Following my campaign, I was offered the opportunity to represent the Palm Oil Action Group at the 2012 Roundtable for Sustainable Palm Oil conference in Sydney. Flying back to Adelaide, looking at my notes and seeing the badge with my name on it, I felt proud to have stuck to my childhood dreams. I remember being so thankful to have had the support of my dad at that moment because, without his help, I don't know if I would have been brave enough to stand up to a national corporation on my own.

Chasing fears

Like this time in my life, chasing fears has always worked out to be a beneficial experience. At a conference on private land conservation in 2019, I attended a workshop on something I had no experience with but wanted to learn more about as it was an increasingly important subject. I was so scared to join a table in fear of the ridicule of the people alongside me who would soon realise I would be no help in the activities set for us. The thing is though, nobody cared who I was or what my skills were and as well as learning a whole lot, I actually could contribute to the task. That experience highlighted for me that I have probably failed more in life by missing opportunities due to fear, rather than taking opportunities and messing them up. As they say, you only miss the chances you don't take.

Take this message home

I feel like the topics I have discussed surrounding failure don't just apply to conservationists, but they should apply to everyone. Team leaders should be providing environments for their staff to grow and learn from failure and people should feel less of a stigma associated with chasing fears to obtain new knowledge, experiences, and skills. No matter how high the stakes are for funding and opportunities for resources, everyone should have the same opportunity to grow and excel in their line of work, both professionally and personally. Everyone should feel supported to achieve their goals by those surrounding them in their lives.

If you see a lonely conservationist, remind them that protecting the natural world is not a burden for their shoulders to bear. There are many dedicated and passionate individuals out there who are all doing their part to help to conserve species and habitat too. Remind them that it's OK to fail, OK to make mistakes, and definitely OK to learn and grow from them. Being imperfect is normal, and the proof is that we are all results of a long line of evolutionary mutations.

If you are in a management position and can shake up the culture of your workplace, consider your staff and how willing they are to come forward with issues and concerns. Maybe it's time for a personal development day, training session or just a simple staff meeting to work on developing trust and a failure-positive attitude in your place of work.

Lastly, if you are in a working position, such as the ones that Lisa and I were involved in, it is time to move on. No amount of job promises are worth the degradation or loss of your value and wellbeing. You are too valuable to be strung along by dangling carrots while you carry on tasks that you were not hired to do, or take abuse from people when you don't deserve it. There are better bosses and better opportunities for you around the corner, I promise. To prove this to you, my last two bosses, as well as my current boss at the time of writing, have expressed interest in supporting me personally as well as professionally and they excitedly share my magazine articles instead of punishing me for pursuing my own opportunities. These are the kinds of work environments that we all deserve.

| 5 |

Let me see your skills. Let you see my what?

The call that changed it all

I once had a phone call that changed my entire perspective of conservationists, including how I see myself. To set the scene: I had been working for months within the incubator program that I had mentioned in a previous chapter, on something that I hoped would transform *Lonely Conservationists* into a business that could help to create job opportunities for myself as well as others in my community. Of course, at the time I hadn't realised how wrong the business structure or metrics of success were for *Lonely Conservationists.*

I was sitting on the couch in a pit of despair while feeling as if nothing made sense in this format for my community, and wondering how I could make it fit. I also had nobody to bounce ideas off of as I was a team of one and I felt very under-equipped to even be in the program. I had never done anything remotely "businessy" before and for the whole duration of the program, I was riddled with fear, apprehension, and of course, impostor syndrome.

Relying on my community to be my team, I reached out to a fellow lonely conservationist to ask for her advice and she kindly offered to chat with me at any time over the phone if I ever felt like I needed to bounce ideas off of her. We arranged a call but I remember being so nervous and sad about the whole project that I almost cancelled- but I didn't. I listened to her English accent over the receiver and was taken by surprise at her enthusiasm and eager advice. I told her that I was struggling with this program because I was 'just a conservationist' and what she said next changed my life.

Nobody is ever "just a conservationist"

"Think about how many skills conservationists have", she said. I thought about my first aid training and how I can conduct risk assessments to make sure that I and others are working in a safe field site. I then thought about my experience with outdoor restoration work including chemical handling for weed removal and the use of tools and machinery for vegetation maintenance. Thinking on, I realised I can also conduct scientific fieldwork with behavioural ethograms, transects, species counts, atlas surveys, inter-tidal surveys, and species identification. I can plan and execute projects and write scientific and specialised communicative reports and emails tailored to specific audiences. I can analyse data with software such as Arc GIS, R, and SPSS. I can communicate my findings with formal presentations in person and online, in scientific

and colloquial language. I can use critical thinking to analyse what others say to deduct relevance, myths, and important information. I can organise communities, manage social media and blog sites and I can use communication software like Mailchimp, and raise money through Patreon. I can create and facilitate events, both in-person and online, and have the skills to engage everyone there in constructive conversation and activities. I can meet with professionals in an office, workers in the field, and with people from countries with languages different from my own and demonstrate effective communication and tangible outputs from our time together. I am also a great educator, if I do say so myself, and can teach students of all ages about local ecosystems and their relevance and importance to the people on my excursions. Oh! And I also learnt Bahasa Indonesia, French and Malagasy to help me understand my colleagues during my time working overseas. Maybe there are some skills I am forgetting, but even so, all of these skills have been essential for my conservation journey. At that moment I believed it when she said:

"There is no such thing as JUST a conservationist."

She even went through some skills I have never had to obtain such as taking a four-wheel-drive defensive driving course, baiting and trapping, animal handling, animal husbandry, disease, and toxicology applied knowledge and skills.... the list goes on. I told her I needed this reminder that there is no such thing as *"just a conservationist"* and I was not, and am not *"just"* anything.

Jack of all trades

I think the demands and expectations of the conservation world are not often considered by your average Joe, to the extent that conservationists themselves don't often stop to consider just how many diverse skills they have accumulated over the years. Conservation isn't a career whereby people ask what you do and then follow their answer up with:

"Wow! The number of skills and knowledge you have had to accumulate and apply to your work is insane!".

In fact, they will probably instead be either:

1. Distracted by the cute animal you mentioned you worked with
2. Horrified by the not-so-cute animal you mentioned you worked with
3. Instantly shut off because they think you're a *"greenie"* or *"hippie"* type
4. Be confused because nothing you described even fits into the realm of a job to them
5. Or be totally lost because they have never heard of a 'conservationist' before.

Having this phone conversation also made me consider all the burnt out and overworked conservationists trying to establish themselves in the industry that never once considered the incredible skill set they have accumulated. Because applying yourself to so many roles in the industry is so common, I wonder to what extent we just accept that what we know is standard instead of selling ourselves on the skills we do have. Ever since I had this conversation, I have been so much more confident at events and interviews because I had acknowledged for the first time at that moment, how many skills and attributes that I can bring to different positions and roles throughout the industry. Before then, I was consumed by all of the ways I wasn't good enough for job roles or new opportunities and how I was riddled with impostor syndrome. Realising the extent of what I could do, made me confident enough to see myself as someone who was adaptable to change and could quickly learn any skills, programs, or methods that I had not previously been trained in.

Phalguni details her experience of balancing art and science within her blog:

The portfolio I now handle is diverse and challenging, and I'm surprised (and relieved) to find that I really enjoy it and find it fulfilling. My acceptance of my change was as incomplete as saying I'm a jack of all trades, and construing it to be nothing really great. Thankfully, not anymore. Do you know the entire saying?

"A jack of all trades is a master of none, but oftentimes better than a master of one."

Cue, self-image boost. A Jack (or Jill, if you will) of all trades is definitely what I am. And I'm learning to own it. I am at my creative best at work and outside, now. As a hobby, I create art that incorporates elements of different art forms and wildlife to create fusion pieces, many of which haven't yet seen the light of day but, oh well. At work, I've never been more motivated to creatively portray a conservation success story and illustrate some powerful figures that popped out at me from the data.

I now accept I'm a package deal and not just one label or title. That I wear many hats and change them as per the requirement or occasion. For the longest time, I felt like an imposter and sometimes on bad days, I still do. But then again, don't we all? Personally, I have yet to meet someone who doesn't have the same doubts or fears or insecurities, and I realised I wasn't alone only once I started talking to others. It helped widen my horizon, and normalise the doubts and insecurities a whole lot of us deal with every day. What was once a huge, identity-crushing thing for me, became something not unique to me and in the process of normalising it, it lost its crippling hold over me.

Taking a winding path

Another stigma comes to those who have taken non-traditional pathways to their life in conservation, having come from backgrounds or degrees in cognitive neuroscience or international relations instead of a conservation-related degree. The thing is though, as conservation is such a broad all-encompassing field, the skills picked up in other fields can easily be applied and could even give you an advantage when entering the industry.

To give you an example of this, I will share with you a story of romance- but I swear it's relevant. When I first started dating my now-husband Todd, I shared with him that we could not be together as I was soon off to spend six months in North Sumatra. Little did I know, I would soon be the star of a rom-com fantasy when he proceeded to quit his job, get his very first passport, and fly over to spend the last four months of my degree with me in Indonesia. Although I was very overwhelmed at this beautiful display of love, I was also concerned about what Todd would even do with himself in a developing country for four months, so I decided to put him to work to protect North Sumatra's rainforests.

The interesting and useful characteristic about Todd is his passion for technology, and specifically his retained ability to tinker which has been lost in many throughout this modern era of easily replacing broken objects. I talked with my Indonesian boss about Todd's skills and he agreed that they could be extremely useful in using drones to survey the restored forest landscapes to determine growth rates, deforestation, and orangutan nests in amongst the canopy. As soon as Todd arrived in the office, he had a drone in his hand and a bunch of the office staff surrounding him on the back lawn. Before long, he was teaching the field staff and the National Parks Department how to operate the drones in the restoration sites and purchasing parts to fix and improve the drones as needed.

The year after we returned to Australia, I found myself

working on a big beautiful property in Kangaroo Valley, New South Wales, and decided that I wanted to document every bird on the property. I told Todd about this dream of mine, and how I wished I had a camera to be able to identify the bird species that I saw, using a field guide for image comparison. Using his knowledge of cameras and photography, he showed me a camera that he thought would be perfect for my birding needs that was within budget and not too tricky to use. That weekend, I went to the shops and purchased that exact camera which instantly spawned my love of bird photography, a hobby that I still partake in regularly to this day. Using the camera, I was also able to document the exact species I saw and use the pictures for making identification guides and educational material for my work on the property.

Todd would never introduce himself as a conservationist or even consider himself one, but his skills and knowledge in understanding different technologies have allowed him to solve many conservationist's problems that they didn't have the knowledge, skills, or time to solve themselves. He is constantly providing innovative solutions and novel perspectives to problems that my friends or I have regarding our work, and I am grateful for the symbiosis that is shared between our two interests and the conjoined application of both of our skills and knowledge.

I share this information not to brag about my useful relationship, but to showcase the way that anybody can apply their skills to the field of wildlife and ecosystem conservation. I believe that you don't have to have a degree or a specific job to be a conservationist because anyone can use their skills and knowledge to contribute to the cause, just like Todd does. I also think that if people outside of the industry share their experiences in conservation and normalise the importance of conserving our natural planet, it can make conservation accessible and relevant to those who otherwise may not know or care about it.

Todd's first job in Melbourne involved working in an office with very closed-minded, misogynistic, upper-middle-class men who would scoff at the news when an environmental phenomenon, minorities, or welfare citizens appeared on the break room television screen. I have heard him tell stories of breaking down these stigmas over the time that he was working in that office, where he shared his experiences of living amongst the oil palm plantations, spending time with our LGBTQIA+ friends, and explaining that his fiancé (at the time) needed to rely on government subsidies. Since hearing Todd's personal recounts, his workmates have been able to see the other side of the coin and understand situations that are outside of their lived experiences. More so, Todd saw his colleagues noticeably change the way they spoke over time. This is possibly Todd's most important role in conservation as he can educate those small pockets of people that we "greenies" could never get through to. I can only hope that Todd's words and actions ripple outward through the people he talks to and that they can show the same level of understanding and empathy to those in their lives too.

Take this message home

If you aren't a "purist" conservationist and you work or

study in another industry, or even if your friends and family sit outside of environmental circles, you have an extremely important role to play in society and the conservation movement as a whole. I need to take the time to thank you for doing the work in educating others and for helping people that went straight from a conservation degree into volunteering or working in the field. By applying your honed skills and knowledge in other areas that people such as myself do not have, you can create innovative solutions that we never could have conceived ourselves.

To those of you who are "purist" conservationists, take the time to get a pen and paper and list all the skills you have accumulated from your time in the industry, I think you'll be surprised at the sheer amount that you are capable of.

Lastly, to those of you who encounter a wild conservationist, just remember how many skills and how many hours of learning both practical and theoretical they have under their belts. From their Instagram profile, it may seem like they are gallivanting around the world and hanging out with critters all day. In reality, however, they are probably smashing their heads against a wall because they are trying to find the statistical significance of their data using R but the code is impossible and they want to cry. Be kind to them and celebrate these humans for everything it takes to protect our natural world.

| 6 |

Just keep swimming

Facing stigmas

I like to think that I am not impacted by the stigmas associated with mental health, but in reality, I think many conservationists, including myself, have grappled quite heavily with these stigmas throughout our time in the industry. I always thought that there was no need for me to seek out mental health help as what I experienced was not a chronic illness. Instead, I experienced bouts of helplessness, fear, disappointment, and confusion which ebbed and flowed amongst the happiness, pride, and grateful feelings I encountered throughout my time in the industry.

Looking at my research on the stories told by conservationists in my community, the dichotomy of both positive and negative feelings shone through. The inspiring aspects of our career, be they animals or plants, new opportunities, or experiencing the natural world, were always contrasted by feelings of self-doubt, unemployment, a lack of income, and the sheer destruction of our planet. The emotional language used by lonely conservationists was also very dichotomous with feelings of love and feelings of sadness showcasing themselves as the top two feelings expressed, implying that our constraints seemed to be as powerful as our inspiring forces.

I know of a common phenomenon in the conservation world where aspiring conservationists will leave the country to work overseas in a grassroots conservation project for months at a time using hands-on skills and learning about the industry from the ground up. During this time, they can feel themselves becoming a "real conservationist" and soon enough, they may even develop a great reputation amongst their local community. They could even have opportunities to speak out at events, represent the work they have been doing and feel established in the field for the first time in their lives. This seems so permanent and real at the time until they are on a plane home, back to their parent's house with no money in their pockets and back at square one.

The feeling of doing what you are meant to do and establishing yourself in the field, contrasted with being at home, poor and away from the abundantly natural landscapes, people, and wildlife you know and love is sometimes debilitating. Suddenly, people that knew you before, cannot understand what you have been through during your time away: the long hours, harsh conditions, or strange encounters. They, more often than not, cannot even resonate with the beautiful sunsets over dinner, the starry nights just talking or the symphonic dawn chorus that woke you up every morning. No amount of story-telling describing your life, or pictures, can instil the empathy you need from those closest to you, which makes it easy for the isolation to set in. To deal with the shock of transitioning from an established conservationist to a couch potato overnight is one thing, but to incorporate social isolation on top of it is another situation entirely.

Survivor

When I worked as an assistant research officer on an island off of mainland Madagascar, we had no electricity, no plumbing, no beds, and no Wi-Fi on the island. I had spent seven months talking to people face to face, playing cards, surveying all day, taking naps, and eating the endless meal that was solely beans and rice, all day, every day. By the end of my stay, I was walking barefoot down the main street carrying a hessian sack full of potatoes and wearing clothes made for me by the lady down the road. I arrived back to Australia right in time for the popularisation of the smartphone when every notification would demand the attention of the phone owner, rendering phones as basically another body part to some people who couldn't tear themselves away.

My two friends took me out to dinner one night soon after I had returned, only to sit at a table with me, both silently typing away. I remember feeling so isolated at that moment that I left to go to the toilet, not even having to go, but just wanting to escape the situation. All my previous interactions in the past seven months had been quality face-to-face moments of undivided attention, so to transition to having this cloak of invisibility built by technology was one of the hardest adjustments I have ever had to make. Also, I need to mention the extent to which I was technologically deprived throughout my time away in Madagascar: I thought the new toaster looked like a spaceship when I returned to my family home.

I remember coming home to a similar situation years earlier when I returned to Adelaide from my first ever overseas grassroots conservation project. I had spent the month preparing food, cleaning enclosures, and learning about rehabilitated animals in Thailand that were rescued from the tourism trade. Having this first experience of learning about global wildlife impacts in person and living off-the-grid with people my age from around the world was truly life-changing for me. Shortly after I arrived home, a friend picked me up and took me to this fancy boutique to exchange a dress she had recently bought. I remember feeling the cloak of invisibility for the first time as I stood in the store in my volunteer shirt and camo pants. I wish I was kidding when I say that the shop assistants walked straight past me again and again without acknowledging my presence as if they didn't even realise that I existed. I wondered if boyfriends feel like this in such stores, or if they would at least be shown to a chair. To go from a place where people were heckling me in the streets to take a look at their market wares, to a store so isolating that they showed no intention that they even wanted my business, gave me reverse culture shock.

Culture shock

Because of reverse culture shock, I remember feeling unsure about my relationship with Todd before I knew that he would join me on my trip to Indonesia. I was worried that

I would have experiences that would shape who I became in the future that he couldn't understand if he stayed home in Australia. I was also concerned that I couldn't get the comfort that I needed from him if he couldn't empathise with what I went through. This turned out to be a fair assumption, but to more of an extent than I understood then.

Indonesia was tough for me, although I didn't realise this completely when I was there as I took every day as it came and put on a brave face. When I had stayed there previously, it was purely in the forest which was a very different experience to spending six months in the city of Medan, a notoriously challenging place to live. Being a woman instantly posed challenges to my everyday life. I woke up early to get everything I needed for the day, all my food and groceries needed to be completed in daylight hours or it would be too unsafe for me to go outside and I would go hungry. I would walk to the places where I could get breakfast or the mini-mart knowing I would be yelled at by a multitude of men, heckling me for being white and for having my forearms showing out of my t-shirt. I walked fast, head to the ground, as they yelled *"BULE!"* the term for foreigner, again and again, a reflex for many men speeding past on their motorbikes. I would then walk to the office, work for eight hours, and walk home with no time for any other travel before sundown. I would then stay in one room of the house where it was air-conditioned, to read alone in English which would give my brain a rest from a day speaking a new language that I still had to concentrate on.

When Todd arrived in Medan, I had more freedom to go

out whenever he was with me as I was then "owned by a man" but I replaced that freedom with the fear of being arrested for living together unmarried. This fear was compounded by living unmarried across the road from a mosque. The mosque loudspeaker would blare its sermons five times a day, which, thankfully, I learnt to ignore after a while. It was a shock that first morning though, as I woke to the sermon from the imam as it forcibly made its way through my window before sunrise while I was soundly sleeping.

I also had builders working on the house that I was living in who would look through my windows and lay in my bed-yes, that's right. I found a builder lounging in my bed when I got back from an office field trip. Full of burning rage, I marched over to the office and questioned my boss:

"I DON'T KNOW WHAT IS ACCEPTABLE HERE, BUT IN MY COUNTRY, YOU DON'T LET BUILDERS JUST LIE IN YOUR BED!"

It turns out that this is also unacceptable there, but the builders were convinced that I was some kind of white prostitute. I also had kids light fires on my porch; I had my field staff proposition me; many experiences where I was very ill, and even a time where I had my ankle snared by an illegal snake trap. To top it all off, my horrible supervisor, who I mentioned in previous chapters, was making me cry with every email I received as he constantly reprimanded me with every communication exchange. I also felt anger at the base levels of misogyny that circulate the culture in Sumatra and I was tired of being considered a sex symbol for the colour of my skin, the hairiness of my legs, the birth control I took, or the length of my sleeves.

Sapphire echoes these experiences in her blog:

The placement gave me some amazing skills: I got to see slow lorises in the wild and help with conservation. I got to meet incredible people, teach at schools, and engage in public outreach. Truly awesome. But for six months after my placement, my view was very different from what it is today.

I was desperate to leave, I spent days crying, I felt anxious 24/7, I always felt like I didn't know what I was doing and when I did take charge or initiative, I would knock myself back down (An irrational fear really: my supervisor was a kind and amazing woman and I have a lot to thank her for). I couldn't drown out the noise, and in a house full, sometimes too full, of people, I often felt left out, or isolated and alone. Leaving Java I was bombarded daily with many "How was it? It looked amazing!". Yet I didn't want to talk about it; all I could remember were those moments where I couldn't escape, where everything was loud and I had felt trapped.

The culture shift was hard to process after eight months away. I was back in a world where people didn't look at me or talk to me, where scooters and bikes were not the common vehicles and I hadn't heard a mosque in weeks. That also felt strange. I felt like I'd been picked up out of this world I lived in and that maybe,

the whole experience had never even happened. I used to dream I
was still there and wake up dreadfully confused.

Even though Todd was there with me for four of the six months, he still didn't understand the extent of my limitations and fears as he was constantly praised for being *"so tall and handsome"*. He knew that, as a man, he had all the freedom in the world and could probably get away with anything he had to. When he left to do some work in Aceh for a week, my personal freedoms went with him and I returned to my previous life of caution exactly as before. I did not skip a beat in returning to my routine of leaving before work to do my chores and locking myself in my room when I returned home from the office.

The aftermath

After returning home to Australia, for weeks and months even, I felt very messed up. I don't think I could properly articulate the feelings I had after spending half a year of feeling constant fear, anger and sadness. I was also dealing with the dichotomy of these feelings contrasting with the fact that I was often in situations that made me feel as if I was living my dream life and giving me an incredible sense of purpose. Returning home, however, I was left with the notion that my childhood dreams were no longer a possibility for me to pursue. Because of this, I knew that I had to redirect my whole conservation career and try to determine my new life goals, wishes, and wants for my planet and my future. Writing this now, it seems very obvious why I was not OK. I had spent half a year in a place that I had spent 20 years working tirelessly to get to, but when I was there, I was overcome with the feeling that this wasn't a mentally or physically sustainable place for me to be.

In contrast, Todd seemed to be more confident and happier than ever, sharing his newfound adventures with our friends and family. Because of his zest for life, I tried to follow his lead and rejoice in sharing stories about my time away. I remember this point in my life as the first time I ever considered seeing a therapist but I talked myself out of it.

The problem was that when I thought of seeking help for my brain, I felt tripped up over the first hurdle. In Australia, it is common practice to go to your local GP and get assessed for a mental health plan. If the doctor diagnoses you with a mental health disorder, you may be eligible for rebates on group and individual therapy sessions, depending on what state you live in. Every time I played this out in my head, I was convinced that I would not qualify for a mental health plan. The feelings I experienced following my time in Indonesia were isolated to those six months of my life and not a continuous or chronic experience. The biggest barrier for me in exploring this option was the word "disorder", as it felt wrong to say that I had a disorder after such an isolated bout of feelings and so I decided to power through this turbulent time in my brain on my own.

As an added hurdle, if we aren't earning any money, and we don't qualify for a mental health plan, how can we as conservationists afford therapy? My friend and fellow lonely conservationist had to choose between buying groceries with the last remaining $150 of her PhD scholarship for the fortnight after rent or spend that entire amount on one hour of therapy. When the choice is between satisfying our hunger or being mentally stable, it doesn't add to the quality of our overall well-being.

Righting the wrongs

Following the publication of the first edition of this book, I felt as though I needed to right the wrongs of this chapter and see a therapist. Through exploring these times of my life, I had noticed that there are still feelings and behaviours that impact me in present times, and that this wasn't just a one-off time in my life that I could easily move past. In meeting with many conservationists in the community, I learnt that Post Traumatic Stress Disorder (PTSD) wasn't just a disorder experienced by war veterans and that realistically, many conservationists are suffering in silence with it.

At this time of deciding to seek medical help, I had been recently accepted into a masters program, that I ended up not going ahead with due to COVID-19 related funding issues. Before I knew this was the case, I went into the doctor's office with the premise that I was worried that the experience of returning to study could trigger some past trauma from my time in Indonesia with my past supervisor. I went into the appointment under the premise that I wanted to make sure that there were systems in place for me to undergo this program in a healthy way. This allowed me to overcome the stigma of the term "disorder" and instead use the opportunity as a chance to look after myself within the confines of this specific situation.

That experience was really reassuring for me, as when the doctor found out about what my supervisor was like, he was shocked and retorted, *"Did he forget that he was a student once? That's atrocious!"* In filling out the form to assess symptoms, four years later, it showed that I still experience strong indicators of having PTSD, even before starting the master's program or communicating with my new supervisor much at all. That was a real wake up call to me that I had been harbouring impostor syndrome about my own mental health, that mine didn't seem that bad compared to those around me and that I shouldn't have a chronic disorder because of a trip that lasted six months. To find out that I was, and still am suffering from a long-term disorder was a reminder to not trivialise my emotions or experiences, or compare myself to those around me.

Although I saw a therapist for only a few sessions, I realised in that time that the acknowledgement of my mental health was enough for me to move forward. Once I knew what I was experiencing, it allowed me to find ways to accommodate my brain's needs. Before acknowledging this, it was so easy to beat myself up for feeling bad because I didn't understand why I was feeling bad. By acknowledging that I have lingering trauma, I can now recognise these behaviours and feelings and give them the respect that they deserve.

The repercussions

I lost a friend over an instance where I felt the mental health impacts resulting from my experiences in conservation. I had spent three to four months in a job in rural New South Wales where I was supposed to be staying for the year. I decided that instead of dealing with my feelings after Indonesia, that I should quickly try to erase the notion that I am a poor drifter and reclaim my status as a functioning conservationist.

In the failure chapter, I described the job and the calibre of the management during my time in this role where I was swindled into running the tourism venture and babysitting the kids instead of doing the conservation work that I was originally hired to do. What I didn't mention was the workaholic husband who squirrelled himself away in his study to avoid his family, the alcoholic wife who used wine as her coping mechanism, and their neglected children who would do anything to try and get some semblance of attention from their parents. A few times, this consisted of riding the ride-on mower around the property and screaming, banshee-style. Considering this, you may understand why I spent so much of my time there alone in my room, or outside watching birds. Eventually, I realised how insane these circumstances were to live in and so my friends planned a rescue mission where they hopped on a plane to steal me away in the middle of the night and drove me back through the winding and wombat-filled hills to the safety of Sydney.

I don't know how I didn't realise this at the time, but looking back, it has become evident that I tried to distract myself from my trauma of being trapped in a room to shelter myself from a chaotic outside world in Indonesia, by trapping myself in a new room in New South Wales to shelter myself from a new chaotic outside world. This accumulated to two years of not having relative repercussions for my actions or realistic expectations set of me. I was terrified of everything I did or said because I could not accurately predict the outcomes of my actions.

When I had returned to the safety of Todd's home, back in Adelaide, I was under the impression that because I was back to a safe place, that I'd go back to feeling OK again. For this reason, any negative feelings I had, I assumed they were there irrationally. I had a friend tell me that she was coming over to grab lunch with me, but instead, she took a nap and never came by. I felt panicked to be alone in the house by myself, with the uncertainty of my friend coming or not coming over. Again, I experienced that the words said by others did not match up to their outcomes. After explaining my frustration and hurt regarding the situation, my friend decided that this instance was enough to warrant not being friends anymore. Sometimes I wonder if knowing I had PTSD at the time would have changed the situation, and other times I realise that good friends will be there for you, no matter what.

Professional, or maybe not

I have heard multiple stories of wildlife carers and conservationists seeking support from trained professionals who tell them that they should leave the industry if it is too taxing.

But this, as I have mentioned in previous chapters, is not constructive advice. It breaks my heart that conservationists who do break the stigma and build up the courage to go and seek help are told to just quit the industry instead of being given effective tools to help manage their stressors. Despite my lived experiences and the impacts that they have had on me, I cannot imagine a life doing anything else. Call it Stockholm syndrome, but conservationists are committed to the cause.

The honest reason why my therapy sessions were so short-lived was that it felt like pulling teeth to explain my situation and the nuances of the industry to someone who just didn't get it. This was especially so after spending time speaking with members of the community who understood my situation from the get-go. There was one instance where I was explaining how conservationists may feel about a certain situation, and she ended up as the one receiving enlightenment about her niece who was really into recycling, instead of me feeling like I was receiving the help I needed. I acknowledge that a large part of the process of therapy is finding the right therapist for you, but on deciding not to proceed with the master's degree, I felt as if the information I had acquired so far had been enough.

A male friend told me of his experience in visiting a doctor to find out if he had major anxiety or Attention Deficit Hyperactivity Disorder (ADHD) so he could work on controlling it to concentrate better at work. The doctor turned him away on the premise that if he had a job, were his problems really that bad? Upon hearing this, I broke down because so many men die from suicide each year due to the stigma of having mental health issues and not getting the help they need. This friend had taken six years to work up the courage to seek help, only to be turned away by the exact stigmas that he feared so much, which meant that he never tried to seek mental health help since. It frustrates me that there are so many lives lost each year due to mental health issues, even when the people facing these issues have tried to seek help.

Career constraints

Just like with the plethora of skills we have, we don't usually stop to consider the sheer range of constraints we face throughout our careers. The range of constraints conservationists mentioned in the *Lonely Conservationists* blogs was a long list and contained heavy topics such as death, sexual abuse, and psychological bullying in the workplace. To be honest, it was very challenging to read and analyse the blogs when the people in my community detailed what constrained them in their journeys, especially when I have been through a lot of it myself. The empathy I felt often constrained my ability to read more than one or two stories at a time and fully digest the experiences that the authors went through.

There were quotes like:

> *"Every day I felt like I was trapped in a nightmare."*

or

"Throughout my teenage years, I felt like I was paralysed by feelings of powerlessness."

For me to read these accounts and understand that it was not just me facing gender discrimination or horrible supervisors or harsh environmental conditions was shocking, but in a way, that also filled me with power. Previously I had felt powerless thinking that I was the only one facing these kinds of hardships, but to see my stories echoed time and time again in the words of conservationists around the world made me so angry. I could tolerate it when I believed that I was the only one carrying the burden, but to know that so many others may be crying alone in their huts as I once was, makes me feel empowered to act for conservationists and to help to create a world where they just sleep in their huts, no tears this time.

I think that is the problem though, we all think we are the only ones enduring all of this, and so we keep enduring it time and time again to the point where my research found that one of our most powerful inspirations to stay in the industry was our own resilience. This surprised me and also disturbed me a bit because the industry has fostered a group of individuals who pride themselves on overcoming hurdle after hurdle when a lot of these hurdles need not exist for us. Why are we proud of overcoming sexism, bullying, or not being paid time and time again, only to keep enduring more with every position we take? Why do we have to tolerate the downfalls of the industry with conservationists replacing each other, one after another, rather than the organisations themselves feeling pressure to change for us?

A friend of mine tried to distribute a survey about mental health in wildlife carers to some of the biggest wildlife caring organisations in her region. The organisations replied saying that they would not distribute the surveys amongst their staff as they did not experience mental health issues. Knowing this was not the case, she took to Facebook to distribute the surveys among wildlife carers groups, and what did she find? Five hundred responses showing a very high rate of mental health strains on the industry. The more that organisations push down the mental health needs of their staff, the more their staff have to show resilience as a priority instead of the pressure being on the organisation to change.

Eco-anxiety

Despite our working conditions, *"conservationists are often exposed to the worst of the environmental impacts"* as was quoted by one of the blog authors. Even outside of the conservation world, I have seen the term "eco-anxiety" pop up quite a bit with doctors, tradesmen, teachers, and lawyers also feeling the burden of the ocean plastics, sea-level rise, and heated urban landscapes.

If the general public is feeling the pressure, imagine the constraints on the people who lost their study populations to the 2019/2020 Australian bushfires.

Imagine the feelings of the people who witness their forest field sites decrease in area as the roads fill with logging vehicles.

Imagine the sorrow felt by the people who use their own hands to remove plastic from the stomachs of juvenile albatrosses who never got the chance to grow up.

We understand when people experience grief when someone they know dies, but it is not socially acceptable to grieve the death of a species, a forest, or a juvenile bird. My dad blamed it on a bad day when he found me sobbing in my room over the death of the last Javanese rhino. I was shown from a very young age that it is not normal to cry over a rhino that I never knew and that I was only allowed to mourn those who I had known personally. Because of this, conservationists are left to silently deal with grief and continue to show resilience as they battle the other constraints felt by the industry.

Elena talks more about this in her blog:

Six years ago, I was watching a documentary regarding illegal deforestation in Brazil and Peru and I clearly remember how powerful it was. There was a particular scene in which we witness the growth of a Shihuahuaco seedling and, as time passes, you see that the same individual was there; when the Vikings reached France, when Marco Polo travelled through Asia along the Silk Road, when Columbus set foot on the American land, when Copernicus first proposed a heliocentric system, during World War I and II, during Mahatma Gandhi's nonviolent independence movement, and was still there when Neil Armstrong stepped onto the lunar surface. It was there until 2012 when a couple of people saw it and cut it down in less than 45 minutes to sell it as a high-quality coffee table in the U.S, China and Mexico. More than 1100 years of history, questions and answers were completely erased in less than an hour. I already knew a few things on the issue, but that scene had me in tears.

Burnout

My usual unhealthy cycle of conservation work is to give everything I have until I burn out, get sick, and am forced to rest until I am well enough to give everything I have again. I have been trying harder to manage this cycle in recent years, especially since creating *Lonely Conservationists* as I don't want to be a hypocritical leader who tells everyone to look after themselves while I secretly burn out behind closed doors. I will never forget the shame of listening to myself talk about avoiding burnout on *The Ecoscientist Podcast* while I lay in bed burnt out at that very moment.

I am proud to announce that this book derived from a period of rest that I forced myself to have. For the first time, I didn't wait until I was sick, but instead, I noticed when I was starting to get run down and I allocated a week just to look after myself. I was so surprised at how resting inspired me to get back to the roots of why I started my community in the first place and reflect on what I had learnt so far. I was inspired to channel everything I had discovered into this book as a way to collate everything I have learnt and share that knowledge with others. For the first time in my life, I was genuinely convinced of the productivity that comes with rest and the merits of allowing your body to do its thing, replace old cells with fresh new ones, and give your brain a well-deserved holiday.

Take this message home

If you are a conservationist, it is most likely that you have a first aid kit with you when you go out into the field. It is important to think of mental health help as of equal value to that first aid kit because your brain is as - no, is more - important than your arm or leg if it happens to get injured. It is important for those of you who are brave enough to get help, to share your experiences with your colleagues and to normalise taking care of your mental health. In doing this, I don't mean that you need to share your deepest inner musings with your colleagues; more than that, I believe that it's important to not hide when we are struggling, to be open about seeking help and normalise mental health conversations around the workplace. Conservationists go through too much in their careers to also battle a stigma for doing something to make them feel better.

If you see a wild conservationist, try and be empathetic to the range of experiences that could be going on in their lives at that moment. They could be experiencing anxiety over replying to a single email because of negative experiences in the past, or they could be distraught over the drought impacting their study species but not expect you to understand. If you have ever sought mental health help, share your experiences, normalise the situation, and help them to break down their own stigmas.

I also know that there are conservationists out there that know they need psychological help but feel pressure to present themselves as "perfect" in academia or to obtain or keep a job. For this reason, it is important for organisations to check their work culture and make sure that perfectionism isn't being prioritised over the health and wellbeing of staff members. As long as there is no regulated system in place to help conservationists, allocated counselling sessions, or an open discussion about mental health, there will always be these struggles circulating throughout the industry. If there is one thing I do know, however, it's that I am trying, as I imagine all of you all are, to *just keep swimming.*

| 7 |

How many fish are really left in the sea?

Alone but not lonely

When I was a kid, I never factored a love life into the equation at all. When I envisioned my life, I pictured myself alone in a forest somewhere surrounded by singing gibbons, trees taller than I could imagine and a treehouse somewhere that I called home. As a result, I grew up prioritising this vision over being romantically interested in people, and I assumed that my constant need to travel for work would limit my ability to have a long-term relationship. This explains why I sent Todd a very detailed letter describing 20 reasons why we couldn't be together before I left for North Sumatra, and never did I imagine he would frequent this book so much as someone still very pivotal in my life.

I was not surprised that one of the first blogs that came in after I created *Lonely Conservationists* was about a long-distance relationship and the struggles associated with maintaining relationships and a conservation career.

Jade describes these feelings in her blog:

Rewind to January 2015, four months before my graduation, I met a guy when I was back home for the weekend; he is now my fiancé. On the 8th of March 2015, he asked me out while driving back home after a trip to the Apostle Islands National Lakeshore to see the ice caves. I will never forget hesitating to respond to him and prefacing my answer with "I just want you to know that this field isn't very stable and I want to pursue it whole-heartedly. I'm just getting started" *and he said,* "I know. I'll support you."

That day changed the outlook of my career. Thankfully, my position with the non-profit conservation organization was only one hour away from home so he came up every weekend to visit or I came back home to visit. The reality of the situation, and of how torn I'd end up feeling, didn't come until I decided to never apply to those jobs out west working with great grey owls and California spotted owls after my time with the non-profit organization was up because that would mean leaving him. Leaving him for a field season was something I knew I could handle, but could he? And how would I tell him? How would that conversation go? Would he be supportive like he promised? At least I had the restaurant.

I remember another young lonely conservationist who reached out to me to ask if it's even possible to be a successful conservationist in a healthy relationship. The fact that he even asked that question didn't surprise me at all. Relationships are a cause of uncertainty in young conservationists when they are constantly switching between seasonal positions in different locations, aspire to work in remote areas, or even just focus on a very unattractive species, like, for instance, if they are a hagfish scientist.

Love in the field

It was always so interesting to me to witness the social situations that occurred within conservation-based volunteer camps in my travels. There would be the young teenage flings, the sad middle-aged staff who took to sneaking around with young volunteers, and then there were the people forming relationships with local staff. Most of these relationships and hook-ups existed only within the confines of the camp-site and the duration of the stay of the people involved. Some of these romances, however, end up surprisingly well for people and are quite long-lasting. It is interesting to see the logistics continue to be full of conflict even after the romance is solidified. You have someone from England and someone from America and they have to work out where they will live, if they will do long-distance, and who has to compromise their hometown, friends, and family. There is also the concern of obtaining visas and adhering to the legalities of living in another country. Whether you meet in your hometown and want to travel, or meet travelling and have to go home, either situation is not easily navigated.

Love island

I don't think that the general public understands or even considers that relationships are a factor that causes so much anxiety for some when considering a future in conservation. The fact that someone explicitly asked me if it was possible to be in a relationship and conservation simultaneously, encompasses this fear that many people have but don't often talk about. It's hard as a teenager to be expected to plan out your whole life, your job, what kind of family, if any, that you want, and to somehow act in ways that will allow all of this to come into fruition throughout the next decades of your life.

Growing up, relationships weren't something I spent much time prioritising or even seeking out. Feeling as if it was the socially acceptable thing to do, more than actually wanting it for myself, I succumbed to a relationship in my second year of university. You could tell I was enthused by the situation because I proceeded to leave the country for nine months during our relationship to travel and pursue my dreams.

On my second trip away, I arrived at camp as a staff member with a boatload of new volunteers. Some of these volunteers were my age, so I ended up gravitating toward them as we were all new to Madagascar and the camp itself. I was soon told by the camp manager that I wasn't allowed to be friends with the volunteers as they needed to respect me as a staff member for safety reasons in the field, and for us to bond would allow the volunteers to see themselves on my level. It could not be helped, but I became close friends with one of the volunteers that was around my age. We hung out all the time and chatted as we had a lot in common and it was nice having actual conversations with people without the wall of technology working as a façade or distraction. Throughout my entire stay, the leader of the camp would constantly hook up with the volunteers, despite it being against the camp rules, and instruct my team leader to reprimand me for being friends with the volunteers as, and I quote:

> *"It would be better if I slept with them in secret rather than showcase a public display of friendship."*

I was also approached by volunteers who pulled me aside and tried to convince me to cheat on my boyfriend. They used arguments like *"He won't know, nothing bad will happen, you're a million miles away"* and *"You'd be insane NOT to cheat".* I was taken aback by this mentality because, even though I realised throughout the trip that I was basically just friends with my boyfriend, I would never cheat on him. I didn't hook up with a single person on the entire trip and I contacted my boyfriend shortly after that conversation by catching a boat to town. In the short time that I had access to the internet, we both reached a peaceful conclusion to our relationship but even so, I remained a lone wolf for the rest of my stay.

The mentality of being on a remote island with no way of contacting the outside world creates a bubble of security as if nothing in your "real life" could ever bear consequence to the shenanigans that occur late at night on a random Madagascan coastline. The truth is though, I saw engagements end because of that bubble. I saw heartache and destruction. Out of everyone that came onto the island with a partner over the six months that I was living on camp, only three of those relationships were intact at the time of them leaving. It is sometimes not the circumstances, the travel, or the jobs that ruin a conservationist's relationship but often it's the notion that where you are in that remote pocket of the world yields freedom without consequences.

It's OK though

Since being with Todd, we have lived long-distance many times, firstly for my work, but then later on for his. It was insane how painful long-distance became over time and how I was less and less capable of it the more I had to do it. Being long-distance does have some benefits though, as when you hang out in real life you are often doing other things like watching TV or going out to places, and that consumes the time you have together. Being long-distance forced our interactions to become more verbal which meant we experienced heightened levels of communication within our relationship. This, of course, was made easier by none of us living on a remote island at the time. Long-distance also perpetuates trust in a healthy relationship and the longing for each other while we were away reduced the amount of bickering that we did when we were back together as we were thankful for the mere presence of each other.

Another benefit of a conservationist's relationship style is the conditions in which you might start your relationship. When Todd came to live with me in Indonesia, it was still in the very early stages of our relationship, only a couple of months in. Up until then, we had only really seen each other on weekends and in very controlled situations. In Medan, we instantly saw each other at our sweatiest and smelliest, we saw and heard each other suffer insane diarrhoea, took each other to the hospital and we saw each other when we were at our most scared and our most passed-out at 2 am on the bathroom floor from whatever bug we had. This experience was like an accelerator program for our relationship, taking us from the honeymoon stage to life partners in a very short space of time.

I think these conditions are exactly what build successful relationships that do arise from the field. To know someone at their dirtiest, most leech-infested self and to find them attractive anyway is powerful stuff. The honest and rawness of living and working in a field site means that you get to experience the people in your camp for who they really are. There is no makeup or technology to hide behind so what you see is what you get. Field-site romance is often developed faster than in the "real world" because of the conditions, especially when you may spend every waking hour together.

When I was working on a Great white shark project in South Africa, I never expected that the person that I dared my friend to kiss in truth or dare, would end up being her husband and someone that she would move internationally to live out her life with. I also never expected to be propositioned with a threesome by a couple who I met at another South African project, only then be invited to their wedding on my return to Australia. I know what you are all wondering, and let it be known that I politely declined on both occasions, flattered as I was. I mention these incidents because I have witnessed that it is, in fact, possible to find serious love while working in the field of conservation, and there are many married conservationists to show for it.

Take this message home

As someone who genuinely thought that I would die alone, I have faith that any nervous conservationist out there who thinks the same way, can find someone if they so choose to be a part of a partnership (or a larger group if you don't want to stop at one significant other, we don't judge here). If you are a conservationist who is scared about your future love life, I wouldn't worry too much. Life is unpredictable, a completely wild ride and you never know what could be in store for you around the corner. As long as you live your life in the most "unapologetically you" way that you can, complete with waders and a Jackson Turbidity Unit measuring tube in hand, someone is bound to see the passion you have for wetlands and fall straight in love with you.

If you see a wild conservationist and you think they are incredible, don't be put off by their wanderlust or fierce passion for the natural world. It may be intimidating to see someone already full of so much love for something else, but we have room in our hearts for you too- I swear. Lastly, to all those people who take a chance on us and do something radical to be with us in our hectic lives in remote, developing, or fluctuating locations, thank you. You prove to us that amongst all the exploitation, all the times we weren't valued, and all the times we were bullied or mistreated, that we are worthy of love. We are worthy of a happy ending for ourselves as well as for our planet.

| 8 |

That person over there is a person

Same same, but different

In researching and fostering the *Lonely Conservationist* community, I have uncovered that the body you are in, has a huge impact on your ability to navigate the industry. People in my community have talked about what it means to be a conservationist with different gender expressions, sexualities, cultural backgrounds and abilities and how these factors have added to their challenges in securing environmental work. In the first edition of this book, I focused this chapter on my experiences with sexism. But considering the updated conversations that have been important within our community, I have added the topics of LGBTQIA+ issues, racism and chronic illness to this chapter to have more of the community's experiences represented within this book.

Sexism

I have personally battled with sexism as a woman in the conservation industry and constantly had to fight for my worth throughout years of working in male-dominated restoration positions and field sites. This is not an uncommon story that occurs in many of the female *Lonely Conservationist* blogs, which was not surprising to me after many of my lived experiences.

After working for a restoration company for two seasons, I was not kept on for the rest of the year which I understood as being a result of budget shortages due to a lack of work in the summer months. It wasn't until my third season where I was working with some good friends in the company, that I found out why I was not kept on all year, unlike the male contractor who had started after me. The culprit happened to be the team leader that I was working with who constantly degraded me as the only woman on the team. I was told that he was offended when I responded to the question:

"You're tall, do you play netball, sweetie?"

with

"You're short, do you play mini-golf?"

I spent those seasons working twice as hard, hauling big olive branches, drilling down stumps, hoeing earth, and planting trees, only to be considered less than equal in my team.

Laura discusses her experiences with sexism in her blog:

> *Personally, I work better with teams of guys than teams of girls, so it's broadly fine. Apart from the times when it isn't fine. When people don't treat you like an experienced professional. When you have to be twice as good as anyone else in the room, to get your voice heard. Or worst, when people actively sexually harass you. In most workplaces today in the Western world, there are avenues for dealing with sexual harassment. But my field-work isn't in the Western world, and often your options are limited. Either stay (and suck it up), or leave. At best, harassment is frustrating; at worst, it is actively scary. But the idea of leaving a project because of other people's behaviour is – for me – even more intolerable.*

You've got male

A conservationist from the community who works in a similar bush crew role and transitioned from female to male also experienced a transition into the world of male privilege. As his features became more masculine and his name changed, he was awarded more responsibility, trust, and respect in his day-to-day life. Instead of relishing in this new privilege, he was more disturbed by how obvious this transition in behaviour was and how it was unnoticed and unchallenged by others. This kind of sexism is something that a lot of women just deal with, as its prevalence is so common in male-dominated industries, but I still can't understand how blatant sexual harassment seems to slide by in so many workplaces.

I was on a satellite camp on a small island in Madagascar as one of three staff members. One night, I was asked to watch some of the volunteers at the campsite while the other staff and the remaining volunteers went out on a night walk. I had sprained my ankle on the previous walk and was happy to stay back and rest it with some of the tired volunteers, thankful that I didn't have to hobble through any more forests that day. While the other staff members, the more superior staff being a male, led half of the camp on a night walk, I sat on the porch of the school hall we were sleeping in to rest my sore foot. While I was resting, the local camp help from our island came up to me, made a sexual comment, grabbed both of my ankles, and spread my legs apart. I squirmed loose from the grip of the big muscular islander and hobbled inside to the safety of the number of volunteers relaxing on their sleeping mats.

I tried to pretend it never happened as I thought it was the most professional move, and I wanted the volunteers to feel safe in my care. After stewing on this incident for some time, and experiencing other disturbing incidents with this man back at our normal island camp, I shared what had happened with my camp manager. While speaking to him, he interrupted me to say that he refused to hear this story unless it came from the other male staff member who attended the camp. The staff member in question refused to say anything against the local staff who had assaulted me as he had been a big help in solving administration problems when arriving on the island.

This left me feeling as if my safety and well-being did not have a single ounce of value to anyone that I worked or lived with at the camp, as the local staff member in question still lived in close quarters. I was scared in the safety of my own hut, and I remember feeling trapped in a cat-and-mouse game as he came to my door and I tried to escape him by climbing out of my window. A few years later, a volunteer from the satellite camp, who is now a good friend of mine, found out about this incident and asked me why I didn't tell him what had happened. I reasoned with him that if the two highest men in power didn't care, then I figured nobody else would either.

Fake allies

I thought that by advocating for conservationists and all that impacts them in their work, I would be exempt from continuing to experience sexism in the workplace, but I was wrong. Following the incubator program that I was a part of, I was hired for a contract job by the CEO of the company who ran the incubator program. The entire way through the incubator, he showered me with compliments about how necessary and important *Lonely Conservationists* was, and how it was so vital for the community. That façade shone through very quickly as I took to the field, and experienced his field staff speak to me using sexist language during my work. On asking who to email the findings of my data collection to, I was hit with:

"Just email the boss, you won't look like a bitch or anything."

Knowing that this person would never utter those words to a male contractor in my position, I lined up a meeting with the CEO to discuss what had happened, and how this behaviour is what I am interested in protecting the conservationists in my community from. During the meeting, all that the CEO and his office colleague did, to try and mitigate the situation, was calling me "brave" for speaking up, and suggest that I should have been trained differently in preparation for this job. In the end, it was easier to make me jump through hoops, sign more forms, undergo more training, and adhere to more regulations, than to make an effort to fix the culture of his business.

Even when people claim to care about what conservationists endure, it is often challenging to muster the energy to make the positive changes needed and easier to ignore them. The only reason I stood up to the CEO in the first place was the knowledge that this behaviour wasn't only happening to me, as I had blog after blog submission detailing sexist behaviour in field sites around the world. If I thought this behaviour was only happening to me in this one isolated incident, I most probably would have let it slide.

Lisa shares her experiences with sexism at work in her blog:

As time went on in the office, a co-worker (let's call him Dave) started spending more time chatting with me. Things started escalating from a "how are you" to him explaining his sexual life with his wife and her fantasies of having a threesome with another woman. This was followed by a request from Dave on Facebook, comments about how his wife finds me attractive, and stories about his genitals. Unfortunately, Dave and I had to work closely together in a team with two other men. Dave thought it was appropriate to make me the end of a few sexual jokes which, thank God, my other male co-workers did not approve of. Clearly uncomfortable and completely outraged, I had to speak to Emily about it and be moved to another shift. I did not want him fired, but I wanted to be comfortable at work. Over the next month, I found Dave speaking to our female interns about his showers at work after being in the field. I made it a point to interrupt the conversation but he completely ignored me. At this point, I made one of my male co-workers come outside to interrupt. I stayed outside with those girls for a little while after. I refused to let him abuse the power of his uniform over interns.

Toxic masculinity

I have witnessed sexist behaviour directed at women, but also seen men suffer from toxic masculinity in the community as well. In trying to investigate why less than half of the blogs were submitted by men, I received multiple recounts of men in my community who had been ridiculed by other men following their blog being published. There were stories of men being ridiculed by friends and family for being publicly vulnerable, and stories of receiving backlash to blogs as the men *"had no right to complain if they had a job in the industry"*. There was also an overwhelming fear amongst the men in my community as they predicted that they would face social repercussions for speaking out about their personal experiences, leading to fewer men submitting blogs and being represented within the community. As a woman experiencing sexism in the industry, I never once considered that male toxicity could be a factor that also impacts men. To be honest, I was a bit taken aback by how constrained these men seemed to be by the extent of their own gender's toxic behaviour.

I also notice a lack of men in the zero-waste space or environmental movement online who aren't just posting wildlife stories or promoting their ecological consultancy business. There is one lonely conservationist who was the first male Instagram page I saw to promote reusable bags, veganism, and plastic alternatives and I was curious to hear what he thought about access for males in this space. He suggested that from looking into it, it seemed like women have a reputation of being nurturing, caring, and altruistic and for this reason, they have been socially stereotyped to be more associated with ethical, sustainable, and environmental behaviour. This reputation has, in turn, put many men off of the idea that this is a movement that is accessible to them without fear of ridicule.

Recently, I heard a person ask why there were no or very few eco-conscious products marketed towards men, with the hypothesis of it being a woman's responsibility to clean up, including cleaning up the planet. I have also seen some studies that show that marketing is responsible for men not using these products, as they are more protective of their masculinity. The studies allege that men will be more likely to get behind eco-products if they contain marketing specifically targeting them. After reading many critiques of gender studies, I am reluctant to cite any specific research in this book, but rather, I'd like to provoke the discussion and ask why we need ultra-manly washcloths, containers and reusable bags for them to be widespread in use by the public.

Finding solutions

To be honest, it made me so mad to find out that men were also being impacted by male toxicity as I thought that if it was something that all genders experienced, then we would be working to mitigate the problem together. What I found, however, was that when I asked the men in my community what I could do to help alleviate the impacts of toxic masculinity in the community, they did not provide very constructive answers.

Some men requested that I push blogs by other genders down to further highlight their blogs and normalise being publicly vulnerable and male. Other men complained that women were so supportive of each other in the community and left encouraging messages on each other's blogs, whereas men did not often do the same for each other. What struck me was that the solutions that these men provided only highlighted the laziness and non-willingness to be the solution or help to alleviate the problem they were facing. It also shocked me that since having this discussion, men in the community were no more willing to comment and leave signs of support on their fellow men's blogs. I honestly felt as if the men in the community were looking up to the women, or especially myself as the leader of the community, to solve their problems for them instead of taking the initiative to be the change they want to see for this issue. It makes me feel disheartened to think of all the women standing up to people who have sexually harassed them or put them down, only to be left unheard. It seems that a lot of men who experience toxic masculinity don't even try to remedy the hurtful actions and thus perpetuate the behaviour. This of course is just an observation limited to my community, but I wouldn't be surprised if perceptions such as these spanned further than I could investigate in this framework.

LGBTQIA+

There are also concerns from non-binary folk within the community that there is no representation for them in the space, and nobody for them to aspire to be like in the same way that boys can aspire to be like Steve Irwin and girls can aspire to be like Jane Goodall. I hope that the non-binary folk in my community rise as the inspirational figures that I see that they are within the community and help to make an accessible space for all the future non-binary conservationists out there.

I know how unsafe it is for non-binary folk, transitioning individuals, as well as a lot of LGBTQIA+ conservationists out in their field sites and I hope that one day they don't have to take as many safety measures as they currently need to in the field.

Theia mentions this fear in her blog:

> When I wander in the woods, I usually make sure at least one person knows where I'm going or wait until a friend can come with me. If I wear makeup and feminine jewellery, I avoid the more rural areas.
>
> One of the most peaceful experiences is to be alone in nature, which is a privilege that many genders, sexualities, and people of colour do not get to relish, in full relaxation. For many, however, nature can also be a strong force in healing, grounding and acceptance.

Matthew describes his experiences of being gay in a country town and how coming to terms with himself brought him closer to nature:

> When I reached my teens realised that I was gay. The confusing realisation came about because I was starting to find the same sex attractive, but also because other kids were picking up on it and the bullying had begun. Small/ rural towns can be cruel places when you sit outside of the cookie-cutter of what's expected of you. After being called a "f***ot" a few too many times, I made the silent decision that I was in fact not gay (as if that's

a choice you can even make, right?). This marked the beginning of my years denying who I truly was. As an adult, I now realise that that is an incredibly daft thing to do. If you lie to yourself and others about who you really are, that lie is going to completely warp your sense of self and in turn, skew the decisions you begin making. You can't possibly make the right choices if you're not being true to yourself.

The reason that I bring up these aspects of my childhood/ teenage years is that they were significant drivers for me finding peace in nature. If you're feeling overwhelmed and you go for a barefooted walk through the bush, how do you feel? The voices/concerns inside your head fade very quickly and are replaced with a chorus of rustling leaves, screaming galahs and white-winged choughs chatting away. I still close my eyes when I hear the bird calls of species from where I grew up and take a moment to listen. It's incredible how these noises stimulate a different part of your brain and help to ground you in moments where you feel anything but grounded.

Racism

Straying from gender and sexual identity, it's imperative to mention how people are treated differently in the industry according to the colour of their skin or cultural customs. In the first edition of this book, I was nervous to speak out on racism as a white woman, but since then, I have learnt the value of speaking about issues that others may not safely be able to. In early 2021, Todd and I released our second season of the *How to Conserve Conservationists* podcast which focused solely on issues that conservationists have spoken out about in their blogs, that we had never experienced ourselves.

This proved to be a very enlightening experience as we were not used to the idea of being spokespeople for experiences that we were foreign to, but we were pleasantly surprised at the overwhelmingly positive feedback regarding this series. During this experience, the most powerful piece of knowledge that we learnt was that people such as Todd and I should be learning from and amplifying the voices around us, to make their messages more accessible to those outside of their circles.

During the racism episode, we explored two blogs by Sebastian and James, and their experiences facing prejudice in the field. Sebastian's blog has stuck with me since I first read it. As a fellow birder, I never expect to face the situation that he did on any of my bird observation walks. He says:

> *Summer of 2018. I was doing my bird counts. Just a regular morning walking around the neighbourhoods with my binoculars and clipboard, scribbling any bird I could identify. After two years of walking around the streets, I had developed a small reputation as a "Bird Man". Most people knew that I wasn't a threat if they saw me walking the streets. A kid comes out of his house and walks down the middle of the street with a roll of money in his hand. I don't know where he is going, and I didn't want to find out. Unfortunately, the path he was taking was the same as*

my transect. To add to the series of unfortunate events, it looked like I had been following him for the last 50 meters. One of us had noticed this, the other was too busy staring at birds.

The kid turns around and lifts his t-shirt and, on his waistband, sits a gun. My mind goes blank. I just remember his high school's "Class of 2019" t-shirt and thinking, "I'm going to get shot by a 17-year-old who thinks I want to steal his money. When all I am trying to do is find out how many freaking birds are on this block!"

James adds to the conversation with his blog:

This is not to say that I have never had positive interactions with non-POCs while performing fieldwork or recreating outdoors- quite the opposite, I've had many. But there is no guarantee that I or other POCs won't be confronted with hostility or violence when we go outdoors. Understanding this fear is part of the reason participation in outdoor recreation is dramatically lower among black people and other minorities than it is for white people.

And while we're at it, let's address why a lot of these areas are so overwhelmingly white in the first place. Why are there so few black farmers? What happened to the descendants of the black and Hispanic cowboys and homesteaders that once settled across the rural areas of America? Or the descendants of the Chinese immigrants who toiled in mines and built railroads that stretched across the west? Or the myriad of indigenous peoples who inhabited this continent for thousands of years? Once they lost their utility to white settlers, they were hurried away with violence, and now are assumed to be ignorant city folk by many of those still living in rural areas (or in the case of indigenous peoples, cruelly stripped of their ancestral homelands and placed on reservations). And that is why so many POCs feel unwelcome in such areas.

A lot of people are saying things like "we need to have a conversation" or are asking "what are we gonna do" as if the answer to these issues we're facing are arbitrary and must be determined by some great convention. But to me, they're fairly simple and apparent: We need to dramatically adjust social systems and institutions to be fairer for everyone, and dismantle the institutions that cannot be changed.

The first conservationists

During the podcast episode, I also touched on the racism here in Australia which is predominately directed towards our oldest living conservationists: First Nations Australians. Thankfully, over time, there have been efforts directed toward specifically employing Indigenous Australians to manage certain landscapes and ecosystems as they have been doing so effectively for tens of thousands of years (some records say 80,000 and others say more like 100,000 years) before the arrival of the British. But during the Australian bushfires in 2019-20, it was evident that we need to reinstate more Indigenous land management practices as the way that

Australian land has been managed in recent times has led to a massive loss of life for flora, fauna and human beings.

Like Australia, many countries around the world are starting to acknowledge that Indigenous peoples and sustainability are synonymous. It has been an awful shame for our local landscapes, cultures and peoples that local land practices have been removed from the people best able to conduct them for so long. I have been avidly reading books by Indigenous authors, listening to the stories of Indigenous speakers and using local Indigenous names to accompany my bird photography posts where I can. It has become imperative for me to learn about First Nations cultures and reduce colonialism in my nature-based hobbies and work to feel as if I am genuinely respecting what it means to be a conservationist.

I never truly felt the impacts of racism in conservation until I started using local bird names instead of their English-appointed names. For me, as a birder, I find the English names to be misleading and not representative of the bird species I see before me. For instance, our magpies are not corvid birds but were named after the similar-looking English magpies. Similarly, our robins are not robins and our wagtails are not wagtails as the English understand them to be.

Since using local bird names, I have often had people asking me if there is a simpler name that I could use alongside my bird photography to make pronunciation easier for them. In my opinion, names like Tchaikovsky, Attenborough and my own name, Panazzolo, are more of a mouthful than 'Waa' or 'Bunjil', the Wurrundjeri names for the raven and the wedge-tailed eagle. Seemingly innocuous questions such as asking someone to simplify a name for them is a blatant disregard for the language and culture. It was not until I started experiencing these comments that I started to understand how normal it is to have culture erased for the convenience of others. By using the English names, we have lost the stories of these birds, stories that connect us to their behaviour and place within the ecosystem. To erase these stories for the convenience of Western speech is a grave loss of connection to the natural world.

I am impressed by the way that the Maori names for birds are the commonly used names in New Zealand and I can only hope that over time the colonialism in our language is phased out, especially within the natural world which holds such integral importance to First Nations Peoples.

My body works differently

Chronic illness was the first podcast topic and was one of the main reasons for producing the second season. Two blog authors had spoken out about chronic illness; however, both authors had concerns about having their identities revealed and their future careers impacted. Todd and I thought that if we could speak out on what it meant to be a conservationist with chronic illness, we could highlight some of the struggles that people couldn't speak about through their own platforms.

As many people are well aware, conservation is a very competitive industry and often, people who have invisible or visible disabilities are worried about their ability to find a job that works within their physical limitations. Some chronic illnesses may not be consistent and a person may be able to conduct fieldwork one day, but not another, which may make it challenging to articulate the work that the person can safely conduct. In other instances, accommodations may have to be made to assist the individual in completing their tasks, such as taking more breaks, having an ergonomic desk setup or having access to ramps and lifts rather than stairs. I find it harrowing that Australian statistics show that one in five people have a chronic illness, and yet conservationists are in the practice of hiding their illnesses to obtain work, in fear of being rejected on the premise of their disability or not being accommodated for at work. It is important, when assessing accessibility and diversity in a workplace, to account for people with chronic illnesses and disabilities because if you aren't accommodating for all your staff, you aren't a truly inclusive organisation.

Annabel shares her experience in a blog:

> One of the difficulties in having chronic pain is that it rules out some early-career conservation jobs. I have to be careful to not cause a flare-up with strenuous physical labour, ruling out a common stepping-stone job for conservationists in Australia (field officer). Repeated movements can also cause a flare-up and it's stressful to tell colleagues when I need to rest.
>
> Last year, during my conservation internship, I had the opportunity to assist in potoroo trapping in a beautiful part of southern Australia. About halfway through the set-up day, my pain was flaring up from carrying the traps. Thankfully, my

friend and fellow intern noticed I was struggling and knew that I wouldn't ask for help for fear of letting the team down. It meant the world to me when she quietly took some of my traps and carried a heavier load.

It's also really scary telling a new employer about my chronic pain. One of the first interviews I had after finishing university was for a graduate position at an ecological consultancy. I was very excited until I read the pre-interview questionnaire. In it, the company asked if I had any medical conditions that might affect my work. They also stipulated that if a successful applicant was dishonest in the questionnaire, they could terminate employment. In fear of retribution, I wrote down my chronic pain and it was, inevitably, brought up in the interview. Afterwards, I learnt that in Australia, there is no legal requirement for me to tell a potential employer about my condition. And if I don't inform them, the worst outcome is that I might not be able to take workers' compensation if my condition worsens due to the job.

Although I know I'm not defined by what I can do, sometimes, I feel like I'm just damaged goods. That interview definitely made me feel like that.

Take this message home

If you see a wild conservationist, please be empathetic to their health, well-being, and safety and consider the fundamental ways that the body they are in may limit their growth and success in the industry. Please help to provide them with a safe workplace, learning institution, or home to be the best conservationist they can be. No matter if you're a man, woman, intersex or non-binary, it is important that your gender has nothing to do with how you are respected at work, and generally within the industry. If you know that some of your staff are within the LGBTQIA+ community or may face prejudice due to the colour of their skin, make sure they feel safe in the field, and send people out in pairs or large groups, if need be. For existing or future staff members with a disability or chronic illness, make sure your place of work is a safe space for them, with accommodations to allow each staff member to work to the best of their capabilities. None of us can help the body we were born into, but we can all be conscious about the way we respect and accommodate others.

| 9 |

Everybody poops

What a glamourous life

The conservation industry, from our own social media feeds to the works of more popular conservation icons such as David Attenborough and Steve Irwin, are rife with glorification. Even in between this extreme scale, there are photographers, scientists, and niche conservationists that we grow up idolising since we first uncovered their work in a scientific journal, magazine, or documentary. I distinctly remember being selected to ask David Attenborough a question when he came to speak at the Entertainment Centre in Adelaide in 2013 and just blacking out for the entire time that he answered my question. I had nervously stood in front of the microphone and asked him how he felt about his history in capturing animals for the zoo trade, in front of a large audience of people. As he explained that zoos play an integral role in inspiring kids to form a passion for animals, I remember consciously telling myself to focus on what he was saying in between my fan-girl thoughts of excitement.

I was not surprised at all to hear that a friend of mine

started bawling her eyes out upon meeting Jane Goodall, similar to when I met Jane. I spent the entire car ride home talking about the powerful and moving way she looked at me through the exhaustion of greeting so many people after her talk. These conservation icons are people a lot of conservationists credit for inspiring them to embark on their own journeys, so to meet them is a big deal.

I understand the purpose and importance of figureheads in conservation to inspire and educate those who would have otherwise not shown interest in the environment, plants, or animals. To be honest with you, I don't idolise figureheads in conservation anymore after working closely with a few people that I looked up to in the industry and experiencing that they are just normal flawed humans like you and me. After spending a lot of time with these people during their normal lives, babysitting their kids and eating their halloumi, it made me uncomfortable to see the way people acted toward them. The special treatment they received from others seemed over-the-top considering how many other incredible conservationists there are in the world who deserve equal amounts of love for their efforts in the industry.

The real influencers

Some of the most influential people in the way I have learnt, grown, and discovered myself in the industry haven't at all been the traditional iconic figures, but much rather the incredible and hard-working people I have met along the way.

In 2015, I arrived at the field site that I would end up conducting my honours research on in North Sumatra, Indonesia. As the only woman in the bare-bones *pondok*, or cabin, the words I could understand in the local men's language could be counted on my fingers, and my place in the society and culture of the field site was still largely unknown. I hid away on the top level, waiting for some direction as to what I should do until one of the field staff called for me up the stairs. *"Kamu suka mie?"* he asked. Not knowing what he had said, I took a wild guess. *"Did he say meat?"* I took the plunge and said yes. He instantly thrust a bowl of noodles in my hand and we sat on the floor together with notebooks and pens trying to muster a semblance of a conversation. 'Mie', I learnt, was the word for noodles.

Spending every day in the forest together for a month is a great way to break down communication barriers, it turns out. I went from taking a chance on noodles to being able to chat total shit with my field staff in the forest. I learnt that the word for banana was a euphemism for penis, much like in English-speaking countries. I had to hide away upstairs to laugh when a senior staff member came to visit and asked me if I liked Indonesian bananas. I said that I did but they were much larger in Australia. From not being able to understand a single word to being able to play around with words was a huge achievement in my language development.

In 2016, I returned to the field site to conduct my honours research and I had been practising my language skills back in Australia, ready to communicate better with my field staff and the rest of the staff back in the Medan office. After one of my forest transects, my field staff asked me if we could stop off at the village for a drink on the way back to the pondok. It was hot and dry due to the oil palm plantations that bordered the forest so I happily agreed.

On the way home, I asked them why there were no women at the place we were drinking at, just men. They turned to me and said that it was a private men's gathering and no women were allowed. When I asked about my presence there, they turned to me and said, *"You're different."*

The reason I tell this story is that the proudest moment in my whole life has been assimilating into my field staff's culture, beyond what was expected of me as a woman. Having started as someone who was hiding upstairs because I didn't know what my place was in their culture, to being accepted into men's circles, was really important to me. This process wasn't glamorous in the slightest and the outcome of the effort I put in wasn't showy. To put it simply, there was no Insta-worthy moment to be had here, but my field staff played a huge role in shaping the conservationist I am, and how I operate within the industry. On reflection, this may be the origin story of the community focus that is now at the forefront of everything I do.

There is room in the conservation industry for everyone and I believe that belittling yourself or your work compared to other successful people in the industry is not constructive for your well-being or for global conservation efforts. You most likely don't know my Indonesian field staff, yet they play a huge role in conservation within their villages and their actions ripple across generations. Similarly, you may be largely unknown for your work in the industry, but that doesn't diminish the importance of the work you are doing.

Online representation

The glorification of conservation on social media is one of the primary reasons why I thought I was alone in my experiences in the conservation industry. In a world where everyone posts the incredible wildlife they are witnessing, African sunsets and diving montages, how could I have possibly known there were others out there who were also crying alone in their huts, or grappling with their rights as a woman in a forest full of men? In times where I was between opportunities, feeling lost and run down, there was no media representation for the grief that I was experiencing and the mental health implications associated with the industry.

Understandably, this is true for most content on social media as many people only opt to showcase the highlight reel of their life. Since starting *Lonely Conservationists* though, I have seen many conservationists open up about their impostor syndrome, burnout and even their experiences partaking in the not-so-sexy aspects of their work, like writing reports and sitting in meetings. I really hope these posts can continue to grow in numbers to showcase a more realistic side of conservation to young aspiring conservationists on social media.

María's blog touches on this topic:

> *And then someone asked,* "Well, are you one of those VSCO-turtle-girls?" *I said,* "A what?!"

A VSCO-turtle-girl is, for those like me who had no clue, a girl who edits her photos on the popular editing app, VSCO, buys scrunchies and metal straws, maybe dons a Save the Turtles shirt and racks up thousands of followers and likes on Instagram.

The question was mainly, I think (read: I hope), asked in jest, but for someone who spends at least an hour on carefully-researched Instagram posts with limited reach, it gave me a lot to think about.

I think this 'VSCO-girl' aspiration is a reflection of a changing environmental movement. It's no longer enough to be passionate, driven, and inspired to conserve and protect for the sake of conserving and protecting. Conservation and the eco-movement are being undermined by people and companies who tout consumerism of the latest (and often most expensive) gadgets, that without, people will feel as if they aren't doing all they can to make a change. Greenwashing, or using hot-button words like 'green', 'eco' or 'natural', trick people into thinking that by buying more, they're helping to save the planet. Similarly, those who haven't yet gone on an Instagram-worthy Caribbean "eco"-tourism trip are made to feel as though because they're not in a position to afford a stay at an eco-resort, they can't really afford to make a positive impact on the environment around them. This is simply wrong, and a very damaging side-effect of the age of VSCO-turtle-girls.

To educate or not to educate

There is one conservation issue that is almost impossible to ignore on social media: the prolific phenomenon of individuals sharing pictures of themselves holding or feeding animals. This behaviour is a great free advertisement for the illegal pet trade and other harmful tourist ventures. Though this is a point of contention amongst many, I feel the need to mention it anyway, as there is angst caused by the act of wanting to let someone know they are inadvertently causing harm to animals, understanding full well that they probably don't know the implications of their actions.

In many cases, I have seen people who study conservation and others who celebrate my conservation efforts, post pictures of themselves riding elephants, or posing with macaques in costumes in their holiday snaps on social media. When I try to calmly explain the implications of their actions, it is often met with a defensive answer. I even knew a girl who had helped look after a tiger that was paralysed from the neck down from being tied up for years as a roadside attraction at a service station. Even so, she still went to a tiger temple, a place notorious for drugging and mistreating tigers, to get a picture for her socials. Because of these experiences, it is so hard as a conservationist to see this behaviour online and to know what to do about it. The glorification of interacting with animals unethically and posting it online is extremely prolific, but it has imminent negative implications for the wildlife in question: physical abuse, restrictive feeding, body manipulations, and the death of wild parents to obtain cute photo-ready infants.

Even in real life, I have vivid memories of sitting on a plane two seats over from a woman who was talking about getting her photo taken while holding an orangutan in Bali. I was arguing with myself in my head to determine if I should interrupt this woman's conversation, introduce myself as an orangutan scientist and explain the implications of her actions to possibly prevent her from sharing the photo or doing it again in the future. I ended up running through all the experiences of sharing my concerns with educated people who didn't take this conversation lightly and so I decided that because we were stuck on a plane with no escape from the awkwardness, that I would leave it and not say anything. I still grapple with my responsibilities as an educator and the action I could have taken ever since, not knowing if I had made the right decision.

In the bird community, many of us grapple with this same situation, but instead of posting unethical pictures, it's feeding ducks. I cannot tell if members of the public are feeding ducks for themselves or because they think they are doing something nice for the ducks. I don't know if I should gently approach people and let them know that they could be slowly killing the ducks by starving them, causing wing deformities, or encouraging algal blooms and the spread of diseases across the pond. I feel as if I shouldn't waste my breath unless I have an alternative to suggest for them, but I rarely leave for my daily walk without a handy bag of grapes to offer as a replacement. It is very challenging to walk around and see well-intentioned humans slowly killing ducks, but not wanting to cause conflict by letting them know that. As a conservationist, an educator, and someone who really loves ducks, it makes me feel as if I am the one that is letting the ducks perish for not stopping the harmful actions of others. After my experience in trying to gently inform people of their actions, I feel that nine times out of ten, I would just be causing animosity with strangers.

The misconception of students

When considering the perceptions of the public eye, I also really feel for PhD candidates, who in my opinion, are not glorified enough. They are unfortunately considered as "just students" and are often lumped in with undergrads, honours and masters students in the minds of the public. Realistically though, PhD candidates are actually working a full-time job in academia for less than minimum wage (in Australia at least). Everyone working on a PhD is exploring a novel facet of research that has never been studied before and is battling to publish papers, complete fieldwork, and pass assessments to know that they can continue in their studies. I personally do not have the aptitude for academia and all of the "dick swinging", if I can use that term, that goes along with it. But I respect the multitudes of people that spend four or more years of their lives navigating the ins and outs of publishing, data analysis, and poverty that lead us to have the scientific discoveries that aid the modern world today.

In early 2020, I attended a gender equity conference for the Australian Academy of Science as a Women in STEM Changemaker where every other Changemaker and most of the attendees were from universities across Australia. I tried to overcome my impostor syndrome by convincing myself that I had a novel perspective to bring to the table, but on multiple occasions, I introduced myself as someone from an independent organisation and each academic I talked to instantly dropped eye contact and ended the conversation. For me, even if I was in academia, I wouldn't want to gain the respect of these people purely on the merit of my university or who my supervisor was. How are PhD students supposed to understand the value of their work outside of academia if they are being judged by totally different metrics within these circles?

Glory to me

I truly believe that conservationists are impacted by the phenomenon of self-prescribed glorification whereby we hype ourselves up in our good runs and use these times to set the standard for the rest of our experiences in the industry. An example of this would be the end of my honours trip to Sumatra, where I was speaking at biodiversity festivals and academic conferences. World leaders in conservation were approaching me to chat after my talks and I won an award for my research. Having a solid month of this lifestyle made the following months back at my parents' house in Adelaide quite devastating as I couldn't even compete with the lifestyle, respect, or opportunities of my former self. This was somehow worse than comparing myself to others as everything was in reach, I was living my best life until I just...wasn't anymore. In times like this, I believe we experience grief over a loss of the life we had. To further the disheartenment, these short moments in time are then used as unrealistic expectations for what our careers should always be like. I have experienced my brother go through similar grief in his sporting career with the highs contrasting so starkly to the lows. As this grief spans through different industries, I think collectively we should work harder to normalise this type of grief amongst people who are highly invested in their careers.

How do you perceive me?

Glorification impacted me and my relationship with *Lonely Conservationists* as well, in late 2020, to an extent where I was on the cusp of deleting my social media for good. One comment from a respected community member was enough to make me reconsider my entire platform when he told me that I wouldn't be thought of as a human anymore, the more the page grew. This was the absolute worst thing I could have heard as I spend so much time sharing my fears, failures, and personal stories with the community to normalise the array of human emotions that are experienced within the industry. Thankfully, there are so many supportive conservationists in my community with excellent counterarguments that saved the page, such as:

> *"Why would anyone submit such personal stories to an online blog if they truly believed there was just an emotionless bot on the other end?"*

My biggest fear associated with the community is that I will lose all of my humanity and personability to the people involved, just as it is deeply upsetting to any conservationist to have all of their work reduced to a popular stereotype. It bothers me so much to be seen as a robot figure because the foundations of *Lonely Conservationists* are built entirely on authenticity and the personal experiences of myself and others. I want the members of my community to see that I am giving vulnerability in return for their weekly blogs and that I am not a heartless creator that is profiting off of their challenges. This is the main reason why there have been no brand deals, no advertisements and no exploitative partnerships, no matter how much our community grows and builds a name and reputation for itself. I have created a community based on trust, and it is my vision to always maintain that trust, no matter where life takes us. This is why a comment suggesting that community members no longer see me as a person, but rather a glorified creator, made me want to give everything up, even if it was just one comment.

It is important to consider the reality of what you are seeing whether it be the work of a figurehead, a social media post, or someone who is working in the field. A small comment based upon misunderstandings could have grave implications for the lives of conservationists, may it be the loss of their work, self-image, or self-worth. I urge all conservationists who experience any ignorant words by others to find people in your life who do understand what you are going through, and to surround yourself with them.

Take this message home

If you see a wild conservationist, remind them that the people you see on stage, in documentaries and on social media are just people normal people who poop, just like you-hence the name of this chapter. In fact, I have never met a conservationist who doesn't have a good poop story to share. I believe that poop talk comes part and parcel with the industry, prove me wrong.

It's so easy to put people on a pedestal and feel worthless in comparison, but in reality, everyone has bad days, good days and plain old average days. I find that it's important to stop and reflect on the truly influential people in your life, the people who have supported you, helped you, understood you or led you to be the conservationist that you are today. I also encourage you to take a look at what makes you influential within the industry. Is it your warm demeanour, your statistical skills or the way you clap louder than everyone else at the end of your peer's presentations? Once you contextualise the real influences and the real important aspects of your life, the superficial parts seem less and less important over time.

I also urge you to be kinder to yourself when having challenging educational conversations, especially when it comes to people choosing ignorance over education. Please do not take personal responsibility for their behaviours; it is not you who is killing the ducks.

| 10 |

The power of community

The context of being lonely

Hands down, the most important lesson I have learnt from the *Lonely Conservationists* community is the power of - just that - community. There is no leader without followers, so I attribute the success of the conserving conservationists' movement to the second, third and fourth conservationists who shared their stories alongside mine. The continuous string of blog authors continues, to this day, to validate my reasons for sharing my story in the first place. I have never experienced such a wholesome, positive and uplifting space on the internet, despite the context of us all congregating over our shared loneliness.

Strangely enough, the only critique I receive on articles and other social media posts is people asking how I could possibly be lonely in nature when nature is where they go to find peace and refuge. These people say I should be thankful to be surrounded by such beautiful natural landscapes. But every time someone does make one of these comments, a lonely conservationist will kindly explain that this is far from the sentiment behind *Lonely Conservationists*, before encouraging them to actually read the article instead of just the title.

Even on LinkedIn, a professional networking site, I had someone comment on one of the conservationist's weekly blogs saying that I had no right to be unhappy while surrounded by such beautiful trees. I had to politely let him know that the words he was reading weren't mine, it wasn't even me in the picture, and maybe he would understand the context better if he bothered to read the blog.

These thoughtless and spur-of-the-moment comments are what most conservationists are, and would have been, used to before they joined *Lonely Conservationists*. Social isolation is a huge issue for conservationists as people are so quick to make snap judgments about somebody else's life using only a few pieces of information to shape their thoughts. This can be extremely detrimental to those experiencing natural disasters, bullying or environmental destruction but feeling like they have no justification to speak up when times get tough. These comments, however, allowed me for the first time to see clearly that people aren't aware, and don't try to gain appropriate amounts of understanding before commenting. For this reason, the weight that we often assign to these comments does not match the value they actually hold. The LinkedIn commenter did read the blog following my suggestion and learnt that the blog was written by a conservationist who had to witness big beautiful trees being cut down every day during her research, instead of what he thought was just her posing in front of a stunning sunlit tree. He retracted his comment.

Take a shot every time I say guilt (but don't actually: you might die)

These comments made by internet strangers are one thing, but misunderstanding comments made by friends and family hit differently. It is so devastating when your concerned friends and family try to convince you to get a "real job" or ask when you are settling down as if these are more important elements of life to consider than the small patch of critically endangered moss you are trying to save.

Feeling misunderstood as a conservationist amongst my friends and family, or feeling self-conscious about my non-traditional lifestyle, has led me to experience a whole lot of guilt over the years. I have felt guilty that my husband has had to financially support me at times during my career, and even when I had low-paying jobs, I felt guilty that my lifestyle was inhibiting the potential of a comfortable future for us. Before Todd existed in my life, I felt guilty for working casual hospitality and retail jobs to earn money, instead of spending all my time on conservation-based projects. How awful is it that conservationists spend so much of their life feeling guilty about being able to survive because we aren't aiding the survival of others? Did nobody tell us it was OK to put our oxygen masks on before helping those around us? Did we miss that safety briefing?

From this information, it is no surprise how prevalent *guilt* is as a theme in many of the blogs, but what surprised me was the sheer amount of types of guilt that conservationists face. There is career guilt in terms of not having a job, having the wrong job, not getting paid for a job or not being able to financially contribute to the household. Another common feeling is social guilt, where people feel like they are the problem for being misunderstood, or when others around them aren't acting ethically so they face predicaments of speaking up or not speaking out about it. Then there is environmental guilt that they cannot be personally responsible for solving the world's problems overnight, especially when there is immense pressure to act perfectly. Who really can act perfectly and what even is "perfect"? As empathetic people in an empathetic industry, we are racked with so much guilt all the time that silly comments telling us that we should "enjoy our time in nature" can make us feel guilty again for having any complaints at all.

Nobody's perfect

I witnessed the pressure of perfectionism in a friend of mine when we travelled to the Yorke Peninsula in South Australia, to take her honours data on owl and mice populations in agricultural landscapes. At the time, she ran an Instagram page centred around being zero waste in South Australia and she was feeling upset as she was getting a lot of hate for not being vegan. Even if she wanted to change her diet, medically speaking, she wasn't able to as she couldn't digest legumes, as well as possessing a range of other conflicting health issues. The last night that we were there, she succumbed to the social pressure from the internet to make her dinner completely plant-based. As a result of this, she was up all night with leaky bowel syndrome, which - yes - is as horrific as it sounds.

It is a total shame that even environmentalists pressure others to conform to such perfect standards. It is counter-intuitive to give someone chronic health issues to take one extra step forward for the planet when many other people could be inspired to take their first step toward the cause. That page has since been deleted because of the unhealthy standards imposed on my friend for how she should be living her life, despite the page being based around her positive environmentally-conscious lifestyle. Conservationists have a terrible habit of preaching to the converted which means that a subset of people who are already doing as much as they can to act sustainably are pressured to do more. A bigger impact could be made, however, if people who are uneducated and unaware of the issues were inspired to make their first sustainable change.

Rage affiliated with these standards flowed through me as I read a book that was sent to me about mental health and the environmental movement. I thought I was going to come out of the book with more information to help my community, but I ended up fuming at its contents as it urged the reader to believe that whatever they were doing was not enough.

I thought about all the people in my community who work tirelessly for free or for minimum wage on conservation projects and then dedicate hours upon hours of their personal time to educate themselves and make sacrifices for the environment around their homes. I knew for a fact that there was even a twinge of guilt that people in my community faced when they splurged on a new t-shirt for themselves that wasn't second-hand, even though it was for a charitable cause. I was disappointed in this book for even claiming for a second to be about mental health when I knew the gravity of the pain these messages could cause. It is never acceptable to tell a conservationist, environmentalist or eco-conscious person that they need to make more sacrifices in their own life when instead, they should be told to treat themselves, rest, and keep healthy because they are the ones fighting for our planet on the front line. This book also had a quiz in it to see how many "unnecessary indulgences" the reader had, and whatever you had highlighted from the list, it asked you to cut out five of these "indulgences" from your life. I only had three: heating for my house, packaged snack foods and driving my car. If I cut out five "indulgences" out of those three, I would have nothing joyful to live for anymore, which I don't believe is a very positive mental health message for the demographic of this book.

I was surprised by the professionals that I spoke with at conferences and meetings that confessed to me that they also feel lonely in their positions. Some felt trapped by the lack of alternative jobs, others felt overworked and burnt out and others remembered the struggle from their former years. I was surprised by the feedback on articles that members of the public had no idea that any of us went through these struggles and that they had bought into the glorification of social media that we all portray with our beautiful animal and landscape pictures. My favourite feedback, so far, on the community was from a podcast where the host of *Speak up for the Ocean Blue* shared his feelings while reading an article about *Lonely*

Conservationists on Mongabay, a conservation news website. He discussed how he felt while learning about *Lonely Conservationists* and how he could relate to my plight. He went on to open up about his own life experiences in trying to establish himself as a marine biologist and how others perceive his life to be something completely different from what it actually is. I would be lying if I said that I didn't walk laps of the block listening to it three different times and feeling so overwhelmed and grateful at how something I had created had impacted the life of someone who I had never met. Another lonely conservationist told me that when his name was also mentioned, he listened to it on repeat multiple times as well. Having some recognition for how we benefit the world goes a long way in this field.

The world on our shoulders

In the beginning, when I created *Lonely Conservationists*, I truly believed I had to solve everyone's problems on my own, but in fact, the community itself proved to be enough. The feeling of being surrounded by like-minded people that you don't have to prove yourself to, justify your actions to or feel any guilt about yourself for feels like a breath of fresh air. To read stories of people who have gone on similar journeys to the path you have taken in life is refreshing and validating. To talk to people who have been there, done that and bought the t-shirt, is incredibly freeing and indicative of a world where you can just be yourself and be celebrated for that. It is the power of the blogs, the small localised chat groups and the celebration of people on the Instagram feed, that makes lonely conservationists feel as if they are a part of something, that they aren't alone at all, and that they belong.

It is so surreal to read someone else's blog that I truly resonate with, in a way that seems as though the very same blog could have been written about my life. I once received a blog that almost echoes my exact experience in Indonesia with the same dichotomy of love and anguish combined with the language, mosque sermons, bustling streets and kind nurturing women who cooked me breakfast. Aside from transporting me back in time, it also felt like a warm hug in the way that the author's words vindicated every notion of trauma, every pang of guilt and every moment I spent wishing I was elsewhere, yet glad that I wasn't. In times where managing the work I do for *Lonely Conservationists* gets tough, it is the stories like these that make it so important and valuable for me to keep persevering so that conservationists can feel conserved too.

Sapphire describes the bustling streets of Indonesia in her blog in a way that transports me back in time to the year of my honours research:

> *Picture this: You're on a mountain, a steep mountain. It is 4 am, and you wake to the sound of the call to prayer from the mosques echoing down the mountain.*
>
> *You drift back into a light sleep waking up again later to the revving of scooters as they whiz past the field house towards the farmland.*

You hear the caged songbirds tweeting, then the chitter-chatter starts, and then, you hear more revving of scooters.

You walk downstairs and greet the cleaning lady and cook with a cheery "Selamat Pagi Ibu!". "Good morning, ma'am!"

As you eat your breakfast you smell rice cooking and hear tofu sizzling in the pan of palm oil.

You take off your socks and head into the wet-room. Water is running in the water bath as you brush your teeth, you step across the wet floor, you hear again the revving outside, people shouting on a megaphone. "Ah, it must be Friday," *you think; they're playing sports in the village.*

You hear a rumble of footsteps and giggles as you enter the lounge. "Miss! Miss!" *they shout as several kids pop their heads through the door. You walk out and colour with them.* "Miss! MISS!!". *You tell them in Indonesian you have to go, but hand them paper and pencils and set them a colouring challenge.*

You walk down the hill and jump onto a scooter and head down the mountain. "Buleh! buleh!" *people shout as they see you, kids run up to you in the shop* "Buleh", "Hello!"; *you pose for several photos.*

On your way back up the mountain, you feel the breeze hit your face as you hold on for dear life during the steep gradients of the hill. Back home you hear the revving, birds tweeting, call to prayer, chitter-chatter, revving again, chitter-chatter, dogs howling, revving, "Miss, miss!", *the call to prayer,* "Selamat Siang!", *shouting, revving, call to prayer.*

Making a change

I owe my current career to the people in the *Lonely Conservationists* community. I have transitioned from an exhausted and defeated couch-dweller, to a project manager and environmental educator. I have learnt to value myself and even go a step further and advocate for myself in all aspects of my career. I have asked for higher pay for a job offer because I believed that I was worth more than minimum wage, and I was granted it because they agreed with me. More so, my boss mentioned that my self-advocating led the company to believe in me and trust me, as they could see that I believed in myself.

In jobs since that, I have now been eligible for project management positions because of my management of *Lonely Conservationists*. I didn't realise until a mentor pointed it out, but just because you don't earn an income from the work you do, or the fact that your work is not tied to any official organisation, doesn't mean that you can't sell yourself on the skills you have acquired. Realising this has opened me up to a world of new jobs that were previously inaccessible to me. I have also started noticing red flags a lot earlier, and have been prioritising my and my community's values when talking to any person or company who reaches out. Before *Lonely Conservationists*, I had only exploitative and abusive managers, but since *Lonely Conservationists,* the jobs I take have managers that are invested in supporting my growth both personally and professionally. Using the interview time to interview companies back and taking note of their values and behaviour has saved me a lot of trouble later down the line.

It hasn't just been me that has benefited from the community though. The most amazing story to come out of *Lonely Conservationists* to date has been hearing about a woman from the UK who got a job despite breaking down midway through the interview. It turned out that her interviewer was a lonely conservationist and so, she directed the interviewee to the community, reassured her that she wasn't alone in her feelings and gave her the position. My heart swelled that my community had even a small part in helping this conservationist get a paid position in the industry, and on the other side of the world at that.

Another lonely conservationist said that she was going to be in a position to employ people soon, and from the blogs, has learnt a lot about the employer that she wants to be, and the work environment that she wants to curate. I now believe that empowering each other and reminding each other of our value in the industry has immense power to shift people's lives from couch potatoes to industry leaders in no time at all.

Opening the gate

Gatekeeping is a huge issue in the conservation industry, between individuals and between organisations. It used to baffle me as to why there were multiple orangutan conservation organisations in North Sumatra and not one just one big one. Imagine if all the people from the separate organisations pooled resources and funding together! Imagine what could be achieved for the future of orangutans in North Sumatra if that were the case!

Since growing *Lonely Conservationists*, I have come to understand that this thinking is engrained in the younger generations too, which severely limits their future opportunities. I once met with a student who had the vision of tackling the mental health limitations of conservationists and she explained to me her idea on how to do it. I immediately suggested a handful of people that she should meet with to try and make her vision happen and she very quickly stressed her concerns of other people stealing her ideas and palming them off as their own. To me, this kind of mentality is detrimental because it limits the potential for knowledge sharing, resource sharing and accumulating skills.

In the development of *Lonely Conservationists*, I reached out to as many people as I could to try and determine the broader scope of the issues impacting conservationists from a science perspective, a community perspective, an industry perspective and the views of the public. I can't imagine what this community would be now if I had just kept to myself, but most likely the experience would have been unfulfilling and I would have given up due to a lack of support and broader perspective of the need. To be honest, I remember thinking that if someone stole the idea of conserving conservationists, I would be happy for my problems to be solved, without having to do the work of solving them myself.

Shortly after this conversation, I was posting on Instagram about a book I had read which discussed some nuanced views on the benefits of industrialisation in developing countries about achieving environmental outcomes. I was especially interested in some of the discussed benefits that could arise from the fast fashion industry in terms of providing entry-level jobs for those that need them. Following this, a conservationist reached out to me to tell me that the information that I was discussing should be left to scientists as non-extremist messaging may give fodder to non-environmentalists to justify their consumerist ways. My counter-argument was that more people should be allowed access to broader information on topics so that they can learn more about the grey areas of environmental issues. Personally, if I relied on extremist media articles and protesters to tell me about the environment, I'd be convinced that the world was ending. Knowing more provides more avenues for tangible solutions to problems and a reduction of anxiety over how bewilderingly bad everything seems.

We also need to be considering cultural diversity and including local communities in our work, especially when working alongside spaces where people use the land and where conservation decisions may impact their livelihoods. We need to be avoiding the array of ways that conservationists are employed from other countries to do the meaningful and sustained work of a local. Gatekeeping the industry to specific privileged individuals is overall very damaging to the future of our planet and its ecosystems.

Turn on your listening ears

The biggest lesson I have learnt from this community is that we need to be properly listening to people's stories. Giving someone a voice is one thing, but what is the value of the voice if it falls on deaf ears? We need to be listening to the staff in our organisations and valuing the words that they say. We need to be valuing the opinions and experiences of local communities surrounding our field sites and seriously considering their input. We need to be listening to the people in our lives and showing empathy and understanding when they speak. I have seen the impacts of toxic allyship within the conservation community and have seen how devastating it is when people portray a persona of someone that cares about the community, but then doesn't take the time to listen to what individuals in that community are actually saying.

I am constantly baffled by people who I meet with from big organisations who assume that I talk about my values until a point in which I will inevitably let them slide. They listen to me talk about my values and my reasons for fostering *Lonely Conservationists*, but when push comes to shove, they expect me to either exploit my community for money or exploit my own time for their benefit. I wish that organisations and people within them would truly listen to what I'm saying and understand the implications of my words, wants and desires. It makes me feel like I'm wrong for taking my values seriously, or that nobody truly respects core values anymore. This is especially damaging for other organisations which may be dismissed on the presumption that they are exploitative, but do have our genuine interests at heart.

At a conference dinner in Singapore, I was talking to a researcher from another NGO in Indonesia about how I was so excited when my field staff found baby elephant poo within my field site. I was so excited because it meant there were baby elephants there and that the critically endangered Sumatran elephants must be reproducing. After spending some time conversing, a woman interrupted me from across the table.

"So what you're saying is, you were that excited about elephant poo without even seeing an actual elephant in your field site the whole time you were there?"

I confirmed that this was, in fact, the case and she ended up inviting me to visit her elephant research site in Sri Lanka the following year, as she had never met anyone so enthusiastic about Sumatran elephant populations without actually seeing them before in the wild. This woman taking the time to listen to me, albeit while eavesdropping, allowed me the opportunity of a lifetime to spend the very next year with herds of Sri Lankan elephants and the amazing people who live alongside them. Because of this, I was able to broaden my global understanding of both elephants and conservationists and continue to listen and learn from their stories in return. In a world where we all collaborate, share resources and share stories across industries, species and borders, there is no limit to the amount of incredible change that we can all achieve together.

Take this message home

Listening to the stories of others has inspired me to respond to their needs in educating others on how we wish to be treated in and outside of the industry. This, as you can imagine, has been a huge driver in the creation of this book. If you see a wild conservationist, you could find out anything that I have talked about in all the previous chapters just by listening to them if you can spare a moment to give them your undivided attention.

If you are a conservationist, welcome people into the industry and open the gate for them. We need more collaboration and an accumulation of different skills, knowledge and experience to improve on our collective conservation efforts. Lastly, welcome other conservationists into your life. I have never felt as happy in myself or my career since I found out that others were along for the ride with me through all the ups and downs of our conservation rollercoaster.

| 11 |

We have tried so hard and come so far, and it does matter

Looking beyond the couch

To experience the overall systemic issues within the conservation industry is debilitating. I know this because it wasn't too long ago that I was lying on my couch with no hope or faith left in the industry. When that was my position, I had no idea that the issues that I had continued to face time and time again impacted anyone else, let alone thousands of others around the world. Realising that these issues are greater than my own flaws has instilled a sense of hope in me that there can be a future beyond the couch for many conservationists if we decide to unite against everything that is holding us back.

As the career choices within the field of conservation are so broad, there is no one union, formalised training program or set career pathway that we can rely on. Being in the industry is like reading a choose-your-own-adventure book where we are all just guessing the right pages to flip to, with our good decisions leading us to the top of the mountain and every wrong turn feeling like a dead end. Being in a community at least allows us to let others know what pages they should be turning to, or even what book to choose in the first place. Having each other means that there is an awareness of what goes on within the industry and that we are now aware that the knowledge that the issues we face are broader than what we would otherwise pass off as a "one-off incident" or a "unique situation".

I have already touched on the power that comes from knowing that you aren't alone. Knowing that there are others that I can turn to, others that understand me and others that I can feel safe and comfortable with in life is great. What is even better is knowing that if I stand up and speak up for the issues that I face, it is not only helping me, but I am also helping thousands of people just like me across the globe. Ever since that day that I got off the couch to create *Lonely Conservationists*, I have never revisited that level of despair.

Finding a purpose

I never struggled with purpose, but I often struggled with the pressure of choosing a specific species or ecosystem to work on when every new piece of the natural world that I learnt about drew me in with a brand-new wave of passion, excitement and obsession. I have researched lemurs, orangutans, elephants and birds. I have taken Todd to dinner just to talk to him about cephalopods and how incredible they are and I have lost moments to watching jumping spiders hop around in the leafy understory. I have never been a plant person, but as the people surrounding me in Melbourne gasp at every orchid and xanthoria they see, it brings me in with wonder and intrigue. My Melbourne friends now argue that I am, in fact, now a plant person after I bought a humidifier to care for my plants during winter and started a little veggie patch in the spring.

Finally, at this time in my life, where I am learning from my discoveries about conservationists and their psychology, and pondering what I have been through in my journey, I am overcome with a sense of purpose and the feeling that this is the role that I am meant to play in the ecosystem.

At the beginning of this book, I shared with you my origin story which spawned from a love of great apes. Throughout my time fostering and empowering lonely conservationists, it has been confirmed to me that my passion for primates has not wavered in the past years of self-discovery, but rather, orangutans were not the species destined for me to conserve. As a full-circle moment, I am realising only now that my passion and calling in life is still to conserve primates, but not specifically the orange ones in South East Asia. My calling is to conserve the diverse and magical species that is *Homo sapiens*, especially the conservationist breed.

For the people

I acknowledge that it is very controversial for a conservationist to want to help the species that are having the biggest ecological impact out of any on Earth, and I understand that mentality as I used to be someone who made snide remarks about humans all the time.

The truth of the matter is, however, that there are some wonderful humans out there that are trying to undo the mess that humans way before their time caused and that humans alongside them now continue to propagate. There are humans with such passion and drive to conserve natural landscapes that are left defeated and burnt out on their couches from the limits of their resilience. There are humans in their research sites getting harassed or abused for their race, gender or sexuality and there are humans out there trying their best to ensure a future for the next generations but cannot even afford to pay their bills. There are people of all ages in this world who are risking their lives with no risk pay or even normal pay to help them if anything goes wrong, like coming face-to-face with a tiger in the elephant caves or a disgruntled orangutan encounter. Some people are enduring a life of uncertainty, grief and misunderstanding with no mental health practices there to support them or standardised human resources for their workplaces.

I am, and have been, one of these people for my entire life and it breaks my heart to imagine that all the dedicated youth in the coming generations may have to experience a life like this as well. It isn't outlandish to imagine that improving the wages, working conditions and the understanding of conservationists could substantially increase the positive impacts and longevity of their work. It isn't ridiculous to think that by helping conservationists achieve their goals, that we can, by association, help to protect multiple species, from the Wollemi Pine to vaquita populations. It is not crazy to conceive that comradery in the industry, sharing resources, information and strategies would save time, money and energy in conservation efforts around the world.

In my recent reading and participation in the conservation space, I have noticed a shift of people becoming more humanitarian in their environmental efforts. I think people are finally coming to terms with the fact that if we want to improve the natural world, we have to also improve the conditions of the people living alongside and within it. It is not just conservationists that we need to assist in this way, but also people in developing nations. By providing quality resources, job opportunities, health and security, there will be less pressure on forests and native species to aid in human survival through providing fire, money and bushmeat. The important thing here is that we can't assume what people need and run in, guns blazing, to give it to them. We need to work with people to understand their needs and make sure the solutions are sustainable for their lifestyles.

To the future

A lot of my efforts so far in making a space for myself as a conservationist conservationist has been highlighting the words unsaid. I need the stories and voices of conservationists to be heard amongst their communities and, even more broadly, to their wider networks. I need conservationists to know what others experience so that they can understand what is common and systemic in the industry and what is unique to them. I want them to know when they aren't alone and what they should be fighting for as a community in terms of their rights and values. I want conservationists to stand up for themselves despite a lack of jobs, and to be unashamed when they speak their truth. I want many empowered conservationists who value themselves and their work to set the standard for how we are treated in the industry. I also want individuals outside of the industry to hear their voices and their stories so they can not only begin to empathise and understand our plight, but also help us if they can. As long as everyone is under the false impression that conservationists live glorious lives in wild spaces, nothing can improve for us.

This book is an effort to share my stories that are echoed in the experiences of thousands of others who join me in my community. I hope that by compiling what I have learnt from my community and organising all my thoughts into one cohesive entity, at least one employer, one counsellor, one family member or friend can help to conserve a conservationist in their life. I also hope that conservationists reading this can feel the power of their voices and experiences, and feel confident in using them to make a change for themselves as well as the world around them. No matter who you are, there is power in your ears for listening, empathising and understanding. There is power in your voice for teaching and expressing your wants and needs, and there is power in your actions for showing how you want the world to be.

Growth and hope

In the first edition of this book, I ended it by sharing that I was still unemployed and still battling the systemic issues as a singular person. A whole lot has changed since then. I have since realised that tackling systemic issues is not something that a person can fight for on their own and that even if change can happen amongst a small group of like-minded people, it will probably take time to radiate, and that's OK. Much like realising that there are other people out there working to help conserve species populations and ecosystems, realising that I can just focus on my small part of the problem, and make tangible change where I can, has been relieving. In realising this, I have decided to enjoy *Lonely Conservationists* and everything we have built together as a community by scaling it down and focusing on the sustainability of my own life. I figured, if I can look after my own health, wellbeing and financial security, then I can have more energy to spend with the incredible people who post to the blog and reach out on social media.

I had my first project management interview shortly after publishing the first edition of this book, and though I didn't get the position, I was stoked to be considered for the interview. It felt like a milestone in itself to have turned defeat and despair into an opportunity to grow into positions that I just wasn't eligible for before.

I did, however, land a job as a bush kindy facilitator soon after, which was a blessing in disguise. Working with passionate kids was a refreshing juxtaposition to managing a community of burnt-out conservationists. I learnt so much from that job about connecting people to nature through experiencing the world around us and I will take these lessons with me through every job I have. This was all amazing until the COVID-19 lockdowns came frequently and spanned weeks and months, rendering me unable to work during these periods. I realised, during my time at home, that I needed to find a position that would carry me through the ebbs and flows of the new world we live in, and that stability, both financial and otherwise, was becoming a bigger priority to me than ever before.

During the second lockdown of the term, I found a job listing that paired my two passions together: community building and environmental education. I was in disbelief! Just a year or two ago, these jobs just didn't exist! I was fortunate enough to get an interview, and I studied harder than I ever have for a job because I knew this was an opportunity that I couldn't let slip by.

A few days later I got a call. I didn't understand what was happening as the interviewer said they wanted to chat with me. It started to become evident that I didn't get the position, but the way they were talking to me led me to wonder what the purpose of this chat was. The interviewer went on to say that each of the panel members felt inspired after my interview. She was told in her degree that only 25% of her fellow students would be lucky to get a job in the industry and so she was impressed and empathetic to the lengths I have gone to make a name for myself in the industry. She went on to say that clearly, I had the drive and a growth mindset and that my only downfall was my lack of management experience within an established organisation. She told me that I gave the successful applicant a run for her money and that if the other applicant didn't have such extensive management experience, I would have landed the job.

It turns out that they were so impressed with me that they wanted to offer me another job that didn't exist yet, that they were about to send out a job listing for in the coming weeks. They believed that if all that I was lacking was the experience, then they wanted to be the people to give me that experience. They told me that they wanted to mentor me and provide me with a professional foundation to help me grow for the rest of my career. As they described the large network that would be available to me, the growth opportunities and most importantly for me, the stability, I was in disbelief that I could finally be presented with the future I always presumed was out of reach.

After 28 years of being a passionate conservationist, with all the ups, downs, twists and turns that come along with that, I feel as if I have finally made it onto a safety boat after years of swimming through turbulent ocean waters. I want it to be known that there are people out there who will want to help you thrive, and will be invested in your growth both personally and professionally. I want to share that being the truest version of yourself, and showcasing your personality, your failures, and being honest about your lack of experience can actually work to your benefit. Since the call, I have seen LinkedIn posts by hiring professionals calling for examples of the projects that individuals have started and worked on, even if they weren't successful. Sometimes, examples of your innovation, drive and resiliency are more important than the physical output that you have produced to show for it.

I am glad to have a happier ending to this book now, as I think that we all deserve some hope for the future. It's truly insane to me to think that I started *Lonely Conservationists* as someone who felt unwelcome and not valued in the conservation industry. Especially now that I have such an incredible community of like-minded conservationists alongside me on my journey, a whole lot of new skills and experiences, and an organisation that values me and wants to help me achieve my goals for the future. It just goes to show that what feels like the end is most likely just a new beginning and that there are always new opportunities if you decide to make them for yourself. Pivoting, changing, taking steps backwards or sideways is still progression. It may not seem like it at the time, but doing whatever feels best for you is probably the right move, no matter what it looks like on your CV or in the eyes of others.

Take this message home

If I could advise my younger self, it would be to stop being so eager to impress organisations to the extent that I would do anything they wanted of me to, just to jump-start my conservation career. Having this mentality and set of behaviours led me to work for unsupportive individuals who weren't invested in my personal or professional growth. Ever since I started being authentic about my career goals, true personality, and the work culture and environment that I wanted for myself, I have had nothing but positive experiences, empowering and empathetic leaders and great work cultures.

You shouldn't have to sacrifice yourself to be a conservationist, you shouldn't have to sacrifice yourself to conserve a species and you shouldn't have to sacrifice yourself. For any reason. You deserve to earn a liveable wage, to be respected and valued at work and to feel confident in yourself as the conservationist you are.

If you see a wild conservationist, make sure that you remind them of their intrinsic value as a person. They need to know that they deserve to be rested and deserve a sustainable life for themselves. If this means getting them some comfy clothes, a blanket and some snacks, so be it! If this means being there for them as an empathetic listening ear, or a warm body to hug, then that is what you must do.

Conservationists: caring for yourself as much as you care for our natural world is challenging and won't just happen overnight. Trust me, I still feel physical symptoms resulting from times of high anxiety. Be patient with yourself, break down your challenges into tangible pieces and do what you can, no more than that. The weight of the world does not fall on to just your shoulders, but we all have a small piece to carry around with us and nurture. In the end, we can't conserve our natural world, unless we conserve ourselves first.

| 12 |

Acknowledgements

I must thank my community of lonely conservationists for the life that they have given me. I am so fortunate to have such an incredibly supportive community of like-minded people who are always so appreciative of me and the work that I do. All the content on the blog (www.lonelyconservationists.com) and the Instagram page (@lonelyconservationists) is curated by the community, and I always admire both platforms with wonder at how people from all corners of the globe have continued to contribute to ongoing content. I feel very fortunate to have had these wonderful people create and maintain such a safe place for conservationists on the internet, and I wish each and every one of them a wonderful future in the conservation industry.

I would like to pay respects to my Coalition WILD mentor Tomasz Wiercioch for being one of the primary forces in converting me from a floundering conservationist to a successful project manager and community organiser. By guiding me through the process of realising my skills, knowledge and abilities, I have been able to reach a point in my career that always felt so foreign and unreachable to me. I have much gratitude for his wisdom, encouragement and realistic perspective that has positively impacted my life, more than words can express. Tom taught me to advocate for myself, sell myself and be the best professional version of myself. I can only wish that every conservationist can find themselves a Tom to help them along their own conservation journeys.

I need to give credit to Rachael Gross who told me to take a week-long break which unintentionally inspired the creation of this book. I know that she is mad that I wrote a book instead of resting, but I am thankful for her concern regarding my wellbeing and for making sure I have the time and space to find inspiration in life. Rachael, you are an amazing friend and I am truly thankful that you have been one of the best outcomes of creating this community.

Lastly, I need to thank my wonderful husband Todd for always being a huge support throughout all the ups and downs of my career. From giving me freedom in Indonesia to saving me from New South Wales, he has been right alongside me to support me financially and emotionally throughout some of the most turbulent years of my professional life. Following the first edition of this book, he became my co-host on the *How To Conserve Conservationists Podcast* and became well-loved and respected amongst the *Lonely Conservationists* community. His insights and contributions to this conversation as someone who doesn't identify as a conservationist have been invaluable and necessary to explore the broader scope of what it is to be a conservationist. For all of his past and future love and support, I have endless gratitude and admiration for Todd and feel so lucky to have him as a team member for life.

Other books by Lonely Conservationists

THE SECRET LIFE OF CONSERVATIONISTS

A COMPILATION
OF STORIES BY
LONELY CONSERVATIONISTS

Compiled by Jessie Panazzolo
Edited by Renuka Kulkarni

The Secret Life of Conservationists

The Secret Life of Conservationists is a compilation of stories from members of the global online community, *Lonely Conservationists.*

On the heels of her autobiographical journey outlined in *How to Conserve Conservationists,* Jessie Panazzolo provides this book as a platform for other voices to add to the narrative of what it really means to be an advocate for wildlife and natural spaces.

In an industry that is often glamorised by the media, this book holds space for individuals from diverse nations to speak on the commonalities of working in conservation around the world. Touching on mental health, isolation and resilience, this is a poignant read that will open your eyes to the un-glamorous world of nature conservation.